# Around the Zugspitze

**Dieter Seibert**

# Mountain Walks around the Zugspitze

## with the Ammergauer Alps and Werdenfelser Land

Selected Routes
in the vicinity of Garmisch-Partenkirchen, Oberammergau, Mittenwald,
Ehrwald, Leutasch and Seefeld

With 53 Colour Illustrations
and 50 Walking Maps in the Scale of 1: 50 000

**ROTHER · MUNICH**

Front Cover:
Weißensee on the Fernpass,
in the background the "Wamperter Schrofen"

All Photographs by the Author.

Walking Maps in the Scale 1: 50 000
Gertrude and William J. Wagner.

The use of this Guide is at one's own risk.
Insofar as it is legally permitted, no responsibility will be accepted
for eventual accidents, damage or injury of any description.

1st edition 1997
All rights reserved
© Bergverlag Rudolf Rother GmbH, Munich
ISBN 3-7633-4242-7
Printed by Rother Druck GmbH, Munich (61151)

# Foreword

After nearly twelve years in print, this volume has become what might almost be called a classic among the Walking Guides. In the meantime, it is a pleasant fact, that as far as walking around the Zugspitze is concerned, not a great deal has changed. The once, almost hysterical boom in new building and development has been, in this area at least, replaced by somewhat quieter conservation.

It is true that the mighty rock massif of the Zugspitze dominates the Werdenfels region. However, this Guide Book intends to introduce us to a much larger area. It ranges from the foothills of the Alps to the north, west to that "Tiroler Fjord" of the Plan See, whilst the southern boundary is formed by the valleys of Ehrwald and Leutasch. However, a view of this massive mountain seldom disappears.

Three elements define the character of our mountain region. The large, impressive and beautiful villages lie, almost without exception, in wide, sunny, meadow-covered valleys. A bright, cheerful countryside – with an exceedingly picturesque backdrop indeed is the effect! The second, ever-present element is the high, light-grey limestone, sometimes as sharp-cut pinnacles and then as kilometer-long toothy ridges above high airy slabs. However, they seem to be far away from the valleys, thus never appearing to be threatening or unfriendly. Water appears as the third element. No less than 40 lakes decorate the countryside. All with different charms – from the wide, open water of the Walchensee, to the "dreamy blue eyes" of the high mountain lake at the foot of the rocky peak. And down every mountain valley plunges a wild mountain stream.

Once again there are three factors which stamp our enlarged area around the Zugspitze as a genuine walking paradise. Firstly, one must mention the network of paths. Almost all the summit ascents in this part of the Alps are on well-marked and prepared paths. Even in the rocky preserves of the Wetterstein, Karwendel and Mieminger mountains the paths and mountain tracks offer the walker a wide panorama of opportunity. The next "plus" is the height of the villages and the ample chair lifts or gondolas with which to reach interesting start points. Last, but not least one must emphasise the beauty of the countryside with all its attractions both natural and man-made.

Sonthofen, Autumn 1996                                           Dieter Seibert

# Contents

**Foreword** . . . . . . . . . . . . . . . . . . . . . . . . . . . . . . . . . . . . . . . . . . . . . . . . . . . 5
**Tourist Information** . . . . . . . . . . . . . . . . . . . . . . . . . . . . . . . . . . . . . . . . . . 8
**Introduction**
  Places of Interest . . . . . . . . . . . . . . . . . . . . . . . . . . . . . . . . . . . . . . . . . 10
  Places of Scenic Beauty . . . . . . . . . . . . . . . . . . . . . . . . . . . . . . . . . . . 13
  Recommended Excursions . . . . . . . . . . . . . . . . . . . . . . . . . . . . . . . . . 14
  Bathing Facilities . . . . . . . . . . . . . . . . . . . . . . . . . . . . . . . . . . . . . . . . . 17

1 Hörnle . . . . . . . . . . . . . . . . . . . . . . . . . . . . . . . . . . . . . . . . . . . . . . . . . . 22
2 Großer Aufacker . . . . . . . . . . . . . . . . . . . . . . . . . . . . . . . . . . . . . . . . . 24
3 Laber . . . . . . . . . . . . . . . . . . . . . . . . . . . . . . . . . . . . . . . . . . . . . . . . . . . 26
**4 Ettaler Manndl** . . . . . . . . . . . . . . . . . . . . . . . . . . . . . . . . . . . . . . . . . . .28
5 Schleierfälle and Scheibum . . . . . . . . . . . . . . . . . . . . . . . . . . . . . . . . 30
6 Hohe Bleick . . . . . . . . . . . . . . . . . . . . . . . . . . . . . . . . . . . . . . . . . . . . . 32
7 Steckenbergkreuz, Steckenberg . . . . . . . . . . . . . . . . . . . . . . . . . . . 34
8 Kofel . . . . . . . . . . . . . . . . . . . . . . . . . . . . . . . . . . . . . . . . . . . . . . . . . . . 36
9 Pürschling – Sonnenberg . . . . . . . . . . . . . . . . . . . . . . . . . . . . . . . . . 38
10 Teufelstättkopf . . . . . . . . . . . . . . . . . . . . . . . . . . . . . . . . . . . . . . . . . . 40
11 Gießenbachtal . . . . . . . . . . . . . . . . . . . . . . . . . . . . . . . . . . . . . . . . . . 42
12 Notkarspitze . . . . . . . . . . . . . . . . . . . . . . . . . . . . . . . . . . . . . . . . . . . . 44
13 Ettaler Mühle – Linderhof . . . . . . . . . . . . . . . . . . . . . . . . . . . . . . . . . 46
14 Kuhalpenbachtal . . . . . . . . . . . . . . . . . . . . . . . . . . . . . . . . . . . . . . . . 48
**15** Around the Brunnenkopf . . . . . . . . . . . . . . . . . . . . . . . . . . . . . . . . . 50
**16** Around the Hasental . . . . . . . . . . . . . . . . . . . . . . . . . . . . . . . . . . . . 52
17 Scheinbergspitze . . . . . . . . . . . . . . . . . . . . . . . . . . . . . . . . . . . . . . . . 54
18 Krähe . . . . . . . . . . . . . . . . . . . . . . . . . . . . . . . . . . . . . . . . . . . . . . . . . . 56
19 Westlicher Geierkopf . . . . . . . . . . . . . . . . . . . . . . . . . . . . . . . . . . . . 58
20 Neuweidtal . . . . . . . . . . . . . . . . . . . . . . . . . . . . . . . . . . . . . . . . . . . . . 60
21 Stepbergalm or Kramer . . . . . . . . . . . . . . . . . . . . . . . . . . . . . . . . . . 62
22 Bichlbacher and Tuftlalm . . . . . . . . . . . . . . . . . . . . . . . . . . . . . . . . . 64
23 Pleissspitze . . . . . . . . . . . . . . . . . . . . . . . . . . . . . . . . . . . . . . . . . . . . . 66
24 Grubig-Fernpass-Circuit . . . . . . . . . . . . . . . . . . . . . . . . . . . . . . . . . . 68
25 Höllkopf . . . . . . . . . . . . . . . . . . . . . . . . . . . . . . . . . . . . . . . . . . . . . . . . 70
26 Coburger Hut and Drachensee . . . . . . . . . . . . . . . . . . . . . . . . . . . 72
**27** Platt and Gatterl . . . . . . . . . . . . . . . . . . . . . . . . . . . . . . . . . . . . . . . . 74
28 Eibsee . . . . . . . . . . . . . . . . . . . . . . . . . . . . . . . . . . . . . . . . . . . . . . . . . 76
29 Höllental . . . . . . . . . . . . . . . . . . . . . . . . . . . . . . . . . . . . . . . . . . . . . . . 78
30 Across the Bernadeinscharte into the Reintal . . . . . . . . . . . . . . . 80
31 Partnachklamm – Eckbauer – Wamberg . . . . . . . . . . . . . . . . . . . 82
**32** Kranzberg, Grünkopf and Ederkanzel . . . . . . . . . . . . . . . . . . . . . 84

| | | |
|---|---|---|
| 33 | Around the Schartenkopf | 86 |
| 34 | The Puittal | 88 |
| 35 | Schönberg or Predigtstuhl | 90 |
| 36 | Niedere Munde | 92 |
| 37 | Reither Spitze | 94 |
| 38 | Eppzirltal | 96 |
| 39 | Mittagkopf and Zäunlkopf | 98 |
| 40 | Pleisenhut | 100 |
| 41 | Hochlandhut | 102 |
| 42 | Seinsköpfe | 104 |
| 43 | Fischbachalm and Soiernkessel | 106 |
| 44 | Krepelschrofen and Maxhütte | 108 |
| 45 | Simetsberg | 110 |
| 46 | Jochberg | 112 |
| 47 | Herzogstand – Heimgarten | 114 |
| 48 | Heimgarten | 116 |
| 49 | Rötelstein | 118 |
| 50 | Kuhflucht | 120 |

**Cross-Reference Index** .......................................... 122
**Glossary** .......................................... 125

# Tourist Information

## Use of the Guide
The Contents informs the reader about the layout of the book and provides a synopsis of the described routes. Important information about a suggested route is provided as an Aide Memoire. Then follows a general assessment of the route and a brief description of the relevant trails. This is complemented by a coloured walking map with the route super-imposed and a coloured photograph. An important constituent of the Guide is the Cross-Reference Index at the back. In this all the mountain ranges, villages, recommended starts, huts and places of interest are presented. Finally, a map on the back cover illustrates the entire area of our interest.

## Pre-requisites
Most routes follow well maintained and marked tracks or paths. This should not, however, avoid the fact that, in parts, a head for heights and a good sense of balance are required. To allow an objective assessment to be made the index number of each route has been coloured. These colours indicate:

## BLUE
Here the routes are generally wide, less steep, well marked with no (normal) possibility of error and predominantly in valleys or alpine meadows below 1800 meters. They can be used with relatively little danger in changeable weather and are suitable for families with children or elderly people.

## RED
These routes are adequately marked. However, in sections they can become narrow and somewhat steep. Generally, they are in higher regions up to 2500 meters and whould be tackled only by experienced walkers with the appropriate equipment and clothing.

## BLACK
These paths, too, are adequately marked. However, they are generally narrow and steep over long sections of the route. They can be in a high Alpine situation above 2500 meters. In places they can be extremely exposed and sometimes use of the hands will be necessary. This implies that these paths should only be attempted by experienced, fit mountain walkers, who are sure-footed, possess a head for heights and who are suitably equipped. The total walking time could be over 7 hours.

### Dangers
Although the routes described follow prepared paths and tracks, care should be taken in places where there is loose scree, whilst traversing steep slopes or where there is a risk of falling stones from above.

### Equipment
Stout shoes with a cleated rubber sole, breeches and a rucksack with a pullover, waterproofs, an Anorak, some food and a water bottle are the minimum requirement.

### Maps
The coloured maps which accompany each described route constitute an important part of the Guide. They preclude the carrying of other tourist or specialised maps.

### Timing
The walking times have been generously assessed. However, they do represent only the *pure* walking time. Ascents, descents and total walking times are given. For circuits and longer expeditions, the timings for individual stages are indicated.

### Mountain Huts, Public Houses and Restaurants
Under the section "Refreshments" all the facilities that are available during the summer for each described route can be found.

### Artificial Climbing Aids
Some walks are described as "descents" from Huts or Restaurants which are accessible by chair-lift or funicular railway. These facilities are often only available during the summer months of July, August and September. At other times the huts etc. can only be reached on foot!

# Introduction

**Places of Interest**

**Oberammergau, 837 m.** The well-known site of the Passion Play attributes its individual village character to the countless murals on the walls of its houses (an art form called "Lüftlmalerei" which has its origins here) and the numerous wood carvers' studios. Of particular interest is the baroque parish church, built by Josef Schmuzer with its richly decorated interior by Matthäus Günther and Franz Xaver Schmädl.

**Linderhof, 942 m.** This castle, with its statuettes, fountains and gardens was built in a remote forest in the Ammer valley as a country seat for Bavaria's "Fairytale King" Ludwig II. Although it is a creation of the 19th century it has much of the baroque and rococo styles.

**Kloster Ettal, 877 m.** The centre-piece of the Benedictine Monastery is the remarkable church with its conspicuous high arched dome. The once gothic building was altered by the master builders, Zucalli and Schmuzer to its present baroque appearance. It contains a finely decorated interior by some of the period's most well-known artists, among them Johann Baptist Zimmermann.

**Garmisch-Partenkirchen, 708 m.** "Bavaria's largest village" is a community which reaches back to Roman times. It almost fills the entire valley floor in the middle of this beautiful high mountain backdrop. The old and new parish churches of St Martin and the pilgrims' church of St Anton should be visited. On a rocky outcrop a little to the north of the village is the ruin of Werdenfels Castle. This family of nobles gave its name to the entire region of Werdenfelser Land.

**Seefeld, 1180 m.** This popular, and somewhat worldly holiday village conceals a particularly beautiful late-gothic church with a finely decorated main entrance and gothic statuettes.

**Mittenwald, 913 m.** Famous for its violin building and its picturesque mountain scenery, it is one of Germany's highest located communities. Of particular interest is the baroque parish church, built by Josef Schmuzer, with its painted tower and frescoes by Matthäus Günther as well as the old centre of the village with its murals and violin museum.

**Schlehdorf, 610 m.** The spacious monastery near the Kochelsee belongs to the Augustin brethren. The centre-piece is the church which was constructed during the transitional period from rococo to classical architecture.

**Glentleiten, 790 m.** An open-air museum which affords a superb insight into the village and farming cultures over the past hundreds of years. Access road from Großweil.

**Murnau, 688 m.** In this imposing market town, lying between two lakes (swimming permitted) is a beautiful baroque church with a finely decorated rococo high-altar and wood carvings. Attractive examples of rural rococo can be found in the affiliated churches of the neighbouring villages, Seehausen and Froschhausen.

*The Schleierfälle on the river Ammer.*

## Places of Scenic Beauty

**Schleierfälle.** This small waterfall presents a very special natural phenomenon. A tributary of the river Ammer has deposited its limestone sediment as canopy-like ledges, forming roofs, caves and small pools. Plunging over these the water is transformed into a myriad of fine droplets like a curtain of pearls. Through its covering of moist, green moss, the Schleierfälle has a particular beauty of its own. Access from Saulgrub see Tour 5.

**Scheibum.** 800 meters north of the Kammerl Power Station (access from Saulgrub) the river Ammer has bored its way through the layers of slanting rock. As a result transverse ribs of rock have been formed on the river bed – a testing ground for white water canoeists. The reddish rock consists of beautifully formed conglomerates; polished round pebbles of different sizes have been baked to a compact stone, in places resembling pre-formed concrete tiles. Access see Tour 5.

**Schleifmühlenklamm.** An attractive walk through a valley with its tumbling brook, tiny waterfalls and rock pools. (See Tour 7.) The small huts at the bottom of the valley were once grinding mills where, over hundreds of years, sharpening stones were manufactured. High above on the Schartenköpfl the appropriate high-quality raw material can be found.

**Partnachklamm.** This 600 meter long, narrow gorge with its, in places 60 meter high, vertical walls is one of the most impressive chasms in the Alps. The gorge has been opened to the public by means of eight tunnels and gangways, cleverly constructed on the rockface. (See also Tour 31.)

**Höllentalklamm.** This cleft is one of the few gorges with a particularly steep descent. The Hammersbach tumbles and roars through a chasm which is partially filled with avalanche debris for much of the early year. Waterproof clothing is recommended because of constantly dripping water. (See also Tour 29.)

**Seebenfall.** A leisurely, one hour walk through meadows from the valley station of the Ehrwalder Almbahn brings one to the foot of the Seebenwände. Here the Seebenbach plunges over a 100 meter high shelf.

**Fernpass-rockfall.** The bizarre confusion of a tremendous, prehistoric rockfall has created this picturesque landscape on the Fernpass. Its debris has filled, what was a valley, to a height of some 200 meters. An especially lovely walk in this countryside of "mini-knolls" is around the shores of the Fernsteinsee with its skittle-shaped island.

**Leutaschklamm.** Here, too, is a rock gorge with smooth, vertical walls and mussel-shaped erosion washed out by the raging current. For some unaccountable reason, the gorge, which is situated due south of Mittenwald, is only open to the public for a short section.

**Großer Wasserfall.** The walk to this waterfall is described in Tour 44. What's special: The stream bubbles out of the rocks immediately above the falls. Unfortunately, one is unable to reach this spring.

**Murnauer Moos.** This kilometre-wide moor is famous for its flora and the complementary fauna. Here, for example, the meadows in June and July are carpeted by iris. The Moor-Circuit, a rewarding three-hour walk begins south of Murnau at the small chapel of Ramsach.

**Asamklamm.** This gorge on the river Eschenlaine is unfortunately only walkable in the lower reaches. A fascinating contrast is the possibility to climb into the partially dry river bed and then, later, cross it at the same place by means of a high bridge. A 15-minute tour from Eschenlohe-Wengen.

**Kuhflucht-Wasserfälle.** We describe this little torrent fully under Tour 50.


### Recommended Excursions

A list of the most attractive excursions follows, with a brief description of each. These can be reached either on foot, by car or lift as the case may be. They are vantage-points which allow an overall impression to be gained or from which the mountains and their grandeur can be seen most impressively. Often there are mountain huts at these view points and one can enjoy the panorama in comfort with a cup of coffee or a glass of beer.


**Hörnlehütte, 1380 m.** In Tour 1 the approach to this mountain hut by means of the chair lift is described. From there one has a superb view of the entire alpine foreland as far as the Staffelsee. Even the Ammersee and Starnberger See belong in this panorama.

**Romanshöhe, 960 m.** The mountain restaurant of the same name lies on the sunny, sloping meadows above the Passion Play village of Oberammergau. A leisurely 40-min. walk from the car park at the Swimming Pool along the "Altherrenweg" through stream-furrowed meadows.

**Laber, 1686 m.** One can reach this steep mountain from Oberammergau by means of the cable car (see also Tour 3). From above the view of the Wetterstein mountains is particularly exciting. An additional attraction is the start point for the paragliders and hang gliders on this exceptionally steep slope.

**St. Martin, 1030 m.** This mountain restaurant lies on the south-east slopes of the Kramer with exceptional views over Garmisch-Partenkirchen and the Wetterstein mountains. The walk up takes about one hour from the ice stadium at Garmisch.

**Kreuzeck-Hochalm, 1705 m.** The Kreuzeck cable-car lifts hundreds of enthusiasts on to this popular area. Using the Promenadenweg, the Hochalm restaurant can be walked to from the Kreuzeck, 1651 m., in about 30 min. All the time the 600 meter high north face of the Alpspitze, 2620 m., is in full view.

**Eckbauer, 1237 m.** This restaurant stands in a beautifully open situation on the Wamberger Rücken. Particularly impressive is the view from there of the Dreitorspitze, 2682 m. It can be reached by using the gondola from the ski stadium at Partenkirchen.

**Pfeifferalm, 949 m.** Some 3 km. east of Partenkirchen, the access road to the mountain restaurants Pfeifferalm and Gschwanderbauer, 1020 m., branches off the Mittenwald road. Fine views to the south.

**Ehrwalder Alm, 1500 m.** The cable car journey to the open meadows of the Ehrwalder Alm (two restaurants) is described in Tour 26. The rust red rock of the Wetterstein and the toothy peaks of the Mieminger mountains ensure a picturesque background.

**Hemermoosalm, 1417 m.** This restaurant, a converted alpine farmhouse, lies on an open, green mountain meadow. Imposing views of the Mieminger peaks (Hohe Munde, 2659 m.) with its high north faces. Drive in and access route (40 min.) see Tour 35.

**Rauthhütte, 1605 m.** This mountain hut stands on an open, grass-covered spur beneath the Hohe Munde. A chair lift from Moos in Leutasch can be used.

**Gschwandkopf, 1495 m.** Magnificent views to the south, over the deep cleft of the Inn valley towards the Stubai Alps and the Kalkkögel are opened up from this skiers' mountain above Seefeld. Ascend by lift.

**Ederkanzel, 1184 m.** From the southern end of Mittenwald, there are several shaded footpaths which climb up to the Ederkanzel and its café. Fine views to the south and into the Leutasch valley are the reward for a scarcely one hour walk.

**Hoher Kranzberg, 1391 m.** Although this is a rather humble summit of meadows and forest, it offers an especially lovely aspect of the Mittenwald basin and its surrounding mountains. For access see Tour 32.

**Tonihof, 990 m.** A restaurant built on the highest knoll of the fascinating hilly country between Mittenwald, Krün and Klais. It offers superb views in every direction. Reached by car or on foot from Schmalsee (20 min.).

**Fahrenbergkopf, 1627 m.** The lift ascent provides an exciting "bird's eye view" of Germany's largest alpine lake, the Walchensee, nestling between the steep forested mountains. A few minutes' walk brings one to the Herzogstandhaus.

**Guglhör, 750 m.** Between Murnau and Kleinweil, the river Loisach is followed by a ridge of hills to its north, on which the farmhouse, Guglhör, is situated. Superb views and accessible on foot in one hour from Murnau.

**Heldenkreuz, 900 m.** This cross can be easily seen on the steep slopes NE above Eschenlohe. It overlooks the entire Loisach valley as far as the Zugspitze and can be reached by means of a mountain path in 40 min from Eschenlohe.

**Loisachblick, 840 m.** Between Eschenlohe and Oberau, the Loisach valley is almost blocked by a mountain ridge. A steep path ascend from Oberau to an open observation platform at the southern end of the ridge (Wettersteinblick). A comfortable 40-min.walk.


## Bathing Facilities

What can be better after a hot, sweaty walk in the mountains, than to wash the dirt and fatigue away in a clear mountain lake – or for that matter in a somewhat less clear pool on the moor. The following is a small sample of the numerous bathing facilities which are available within the area this Guide covers. Naturally, there is, in addition, a considerable number of indoor baths.

**Soiener See, 790 m.** The water in this lake near Bad Bayersoien warms rapidly to a comfortable "bathing temperature". Swimming is permitted on both north and south banks. Most interesting flora!

**Wellenberg.** A large leisure and bathing facility in the east of Oberammergau, offering open-air swimming, sun-bathing lawns, an indoor pool etc.

**Plansee, 976 m.** The second largest lake in the Tyrol lies like a fjord between the steep mountains. The cold water is only rarely suitable for swimming. The best places are to be found on the north bank, near the two restaurants and on the flatter east bank.

*On the Loisach.*

**Pflegersee, 850 m.** A picturesque mountain pool, nestling in a wooded depression at the foot of the steep Seleswände. Outdoor swimming pool and restaurant. Approach from Garmisch on a steep forestry road (15 %, 2 km.).

**Rießersee, 795 m.** A long, narrow lake lying hidden in a small, steeply wooded valley with the impressive Waxenstein as its backdrop. Access from Garmisch.

**Badersee, 770 m.** A prehistoric rockfall, now carpeted by grass and trees, gives the holiday village of Grainau a character all of its own. It also created the tiny Badersee with its remarkably green water that now lies in the middle of the community.

**Eibsee, 973 m.** The small islands and sheltered coves contribute to the wonderful situation of the 2,4 km. long Eibsee. On the south bank can be found an outdoor swimming pool, whilst on the north there are swimming beaches. Generally, the water is cold! The Zugspitze towers high over the lake.

**Mittersee, 1082 m.** Of all the lakes in the Fernpass countryside above Biberwier, the small and relatively shallow Mittersee offers the best opportunity for a – cool – swim! However, the Fernsteinsee, with its especially beautiful banks is also inviting just south of the pass.

**Möserersee, 1250 m.** A lovely lake above the village of Mösern, near Seefeld, which is suitable for swimming during warm weather. Similar, too is the nearby Lottensee, 1277 m., when there is adequate water.

**Wildsee, 1160 m.** This lake, which gave Seefeld its name, lies between the road and the Gschwandkopf. Only during a really warm period does the water reach a reasonably acceptable temperature.

**Lautersee, 1016 m.** Germany's highest outdoor swimming pool is situated on this relatively large round lake. Reached from Mittenwald by a 40-min. journey through the Laintal and its waterfall, or through beautiful, open pine forests. Impressive mountain backdrop.

**Ferchensee, 1063 m.** Some 1500 m. up the valley from Lautersee is the rather harsher lying Ferchensee. It, too, can be equally inviting on warmer days. 70 min. from Mittenwald.

*Eibsee north bank.*

**Grubsee, 905 m.** Of the three lakes which lie between Klais and Krün, the Grubsee belongs to the water rats (outdoor swimming pool!), the Tennsee to the camping fraternity and the larger, almost unspoiled Barmsee with its bulrushes and meadows of wild flowers, to nature lovers who value the birds and the flowers.

**Geroldsee, 935 m.** The impressive mountainous background makes this lake in the meadows near Klais a popular motif for photographers. A mini-swimming facility near the tiny village of Gerold.

**Walchensee, 802 m.** With an area of some 16 sq.km., the Walchensee is not only the largest German mountain lake but with a depth of 192 meters, the deepest as well. Surrounded by wooded hills it has an almost harsh atmosphere. Only during a truly warm spell does the water become warm enough to make swimming enjoyable. Open-air swimming near the village of Walchensee itself, or on the south bank.

**Kochelsee, 599 m.** A large lake, partially enclosed by steep mountain slopes and partly by reeds it boasts a swimming area, indeed a complete leisure facility with swimming pools and water chute called "Trimini".

**Staffelsee, 649 m.** An ideal and popular bathing lake situated some distance away from the Alps. Because it is somewhat shallow its water warms up quickly. Swimming facilities in Seehausen, Murnau and Uffing.

*Right: High forest near the Hemermoosalm. In the background the Mieminger range.*
*Below: The Geroldsee near Klais.*

# 1 Hörnle, 1548 m

Outstations of the Ammergauer mountains, high above the alpine foreland

**Either: A traverse of the three Hörnle from the top station of the chair lift; or a circuit from Kappel via Aiblehütte – Hinteres Hörnle – Hörnlealm – Kappel**

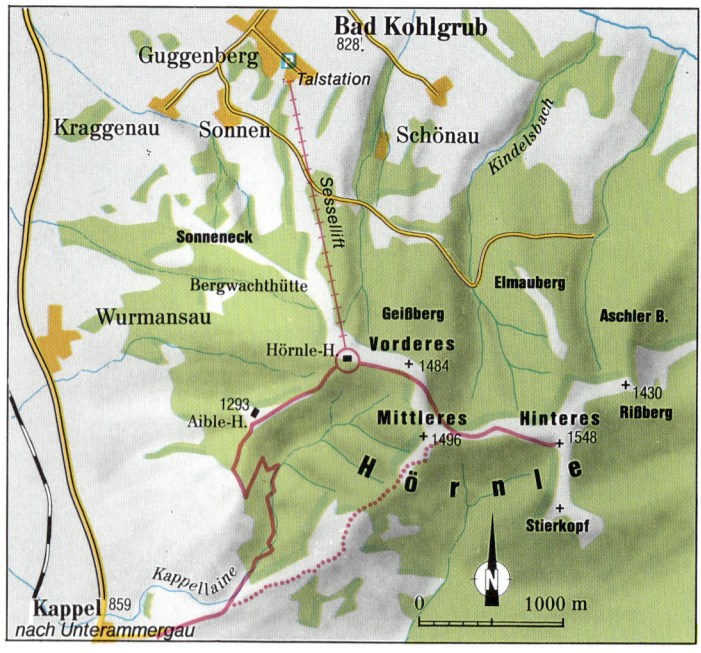

**Approach:** Bad Kohlgrub, 828 m., holiday village and spa (mud baths) on the northern edge of the Alps.
**Start:** Top station of the chair lift, 1380 m., bottom station in Guggenberg, a suburb of Bad Kohlgrub.
**Parking:** Bottom lift station.
**Walking Times:** Top station – Hinteres Hörnle ¾ hr., for a traverse from Vorderen and Mittleren Hörnle ½ hr. more; alternatively ascend from Unterammergau-Kappel 2½ hrs.
**Difficulty:** Comfortable walking through alpine meadows.
**Highest Point:** Hinteres Hörnle, 1548 m., or Vorderes Hörnle, 1484 m., Mittleres Hörnle, 1496 m.
**Refreshments:** Hörnlehütte by top station.
**Of Interest:** Fine views down on to the Staffelsee.

Should a novice, or a stranger to the Alps, ever ask where he, or she in peace and quiet could "try out" mountain walking for the first time, then the Hörnle with its three rounded, grass summits would be a sound recommendation. The path from the top station to the Hinteres Hörnle (the highest) is short, without danger and provides all the magic of a mountain walk, high above the valley with uninterrupted views and a summit ascent which brings that necessary sense of achievement.

Whoever thinks that this mountain walk is too short, should choose the climb up from Unterammergau-Kappel.

**From the top station to Hinteres Hörnle:** The more easy-going will remain on the main path, reaching the grassy main summit by traversing the Vorderes Hörnle to the south and the Mittleres Hörnle to the east. However, both mountains can be traversed along the ridge, too.

**Round trip from Unterammergau-Kappel:** Kappel lies 1 km. north of Unterammergau across the B23. On the farm track, across the meadows to the actual foot of the mountain. Left into a gully leaving it after 20 min. to the left onto the parallel ridge an across – past the Aiblehütte – to the Hörnlehütte (top station). Continue as above to Hinteres Hörnle.

Descend to the saddle between Hinteres and Mittleres Hörnle. Take the path along the south ridge of the latter. Keeping to this path along the ridge then down over high meadowed slopes to the foot of the mountain and back to Kappel.

*Kappel (near Unterammergau) and Aufacker.*

## 2  Großer Aufacker, 1542 m

A round-trip over a quiet and unspoiled wooded mountain

**St. Gregor – Gschwandkopfrücken – Aufacker – Rehbreinsattel – Romanshöhe – St. Gregor**

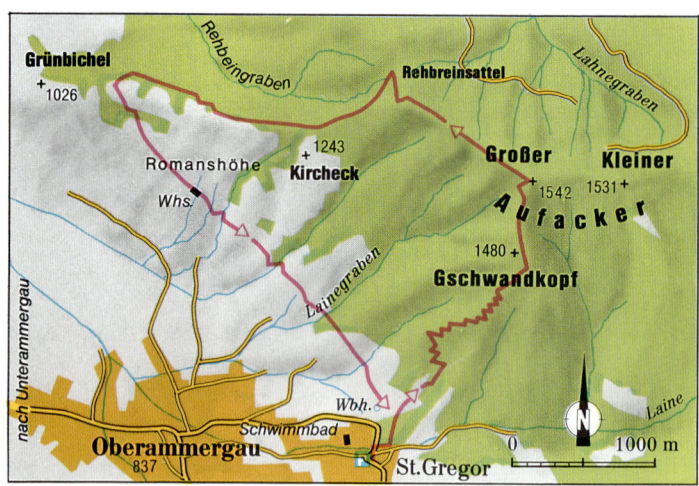

**Approach:** Oberammergau, 837 m., centre of the Ammer valley, known for its Passion Play and wood carving, beautiful baroque church, murals on the house walls.
**Start:** St. Gregor at the "Wellenberg" swimming pool.
**Parking:** Large car park at the swimming pool.
**Walking Times:** Ascent and descent each 2 hrs.
**Difficulty:** Narrow, but adequate paths, in places wet under foot.
**Highest Point:** Großer Aufacker, 1542 m.
**Refreshments:** Restaurant Romanshöhe.

Trees are the dominating feature on the Aufacker. On our tour we are walking for some considerable time on forest paths. In spite of this the route is never boring.
The many clearings take care of that. Several permit an unrestricted view into the valley near Oberammergau, while others are solitary, enchanting places – ideal to sit and dream (these are to be found mostly on descending). Even on top, around the summit, the tall, strong spruces hardly disturb the view.

The descent north to the Rehbreinsattel can become swampy lower down the mountain. Wet feet can be the result of carelessness – however, an especially rich vegetation is the reward.

*Oberammergau*

**The Ascent:** On to the "Altherrenweg" above the car park for a short distance to the left. The path to Aufacker branches upwards (sign). An easily followed path leads steadily upwards (interminable bends). Right around the Gschwandkopf and on to the summit.

**The Descent via the Rehbreinsattel:** The wide NW ridge of the Aufacker leads directly down on to the saddle. Remain in the open strip in the middle of the ridge. On the swampy ground in the saddle sharp left and above the Rehbreinbach gradually left to a wide wooded ridge.
Almost 2 km. on the ridge, sometimes right below it. The path then drops around the ridge and descends quite steeply across its southern slopes to the Romanshöhe restaurant. Then, with fine views into the valley, along the comfortable "Altherrenweg" back to the car park.

# 3 Laber, 1686 m

Two routes on the hang gliders' mountain

**Oberammergau – St. Gregor – Laberalm – Laberberg – around the Ettaler Manndl – Soilesee – St. Gregor**

**Approach:** Oberammergau, 837 m. Centre of the Ammer valley, renowned for its Passion Play and wood carvings, beautiful baroque church, murals on the walls of many houses.
**Start:** St. Gregor, bottom station of the Laberbahn.
**Parking:** At the bottom station.
**Walking Times:** 2½ hrs. ascent to the Laber (alternatively with the lift), 1 hr. to circumnavigate Ettaler Manndl to Soilesee. 1 hr. descent.
**Difficulty:** Always good, but sometimes rocky tracks.
**Highest Point:** Laber west summit, 1686 m.
**Refreshments:** Laber Summit House.
**Of Interest:** Views of the Wetterstein, hang gliders and paragliders taking-off, the jagged pinnacles of the Ettaler Manndl.

From Oberammergau a lift ascends on to this broad massif, which is as well-known for its magnificent views to the south and the Wetterstein with the Zugspitze, as it is for its starting point for the hang gliders, who have their take-off ramp next to the top station. How should we spend the day? There's a lift and two paths and a circuit of the neighbouring mountain Ettaler Manndl sounds inviting, too. We've put together a round-trip which offers not only the maximum in adventure and wonderful views but is also relatively long. Those who wish to invest rather less time and energy can take the cable car!

**The Ascent:** On the forest road or footpath to the forest edge. A few minutes later take the right fork and steeply up through the trees to the Laberalm in its grassy saddle. Slanting right and upwards across the slope to the wet ridge and on a carefully prepared track. Cross the ridge through a narrow saddle passing picturesque rock pinnacles to the higher west summit and on to the top station. Alternatively to here with the lift.

**Around the Ettaler Manndl:** Descend steeply to the SE in a nearby saddle. Then almost level among spruce trees on the southern slope traversing around the Manndlköpfe and to the east of the Manndl itself (summit ascent see Tour 4). To the right around the rocks then over an open slope, finally a short wooded section to the tiny Soilesee, 1398 m.

**The Descent:** Follow the track north initially, then west down the long valley to the car park.

*Laber, seen from the south.*

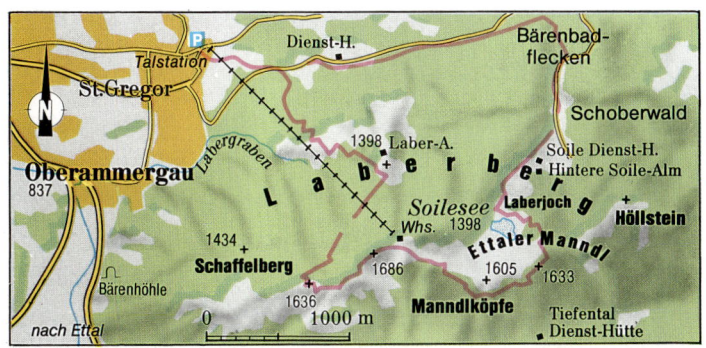

# 4 Ettaler Manndl, 1605 m

A Via Ferrata on a mountain in the lower alps

**Ettal – Tiefentalgraben – Ettaler Manndl**

**Approach:** Ettal, 877 m., popular goal for excursions, famous for the Benedictine monastery and its church, highest situated village in the Ammer valley.
**Start:** NE edge of the village at the mouth of the Tiefentalgraben.
**Parking:** Car park at the start.
**Walking Times:** Ascent 2 hrs., descent about 1½ hrs.
**Difficulty:** A good path to the rocks, then a secure Via Ferrata in steep ground, where a good sense of balance and a head for heights are essential. At weekends it can be crowded with the odd traffic jam at the roped sections.
**Highest Point:** Ettaler Manndl, 1605 m.
**Refreshments:** None!
**Of Interest:** Views of the Murnau Moor and the Wetterstein.

The summit towers conspicuously 50 m. above the woods as a brazen finger of rock. However, the first part of its name is somewhat misleading. Whilst it can be seen from the Loisach valley, near Ohlstadt, from Ettal it can barely be discerned. Ettal is simply the normal start.
Of course one can traverse across quicker from the Laber and with less effort (see Tour 3). A head for heights is essential to climb to the summit cross. A proper Via Ferrata, with chains, wire ropes and anchors provides continuous security up the precipitous face.

**The Ascent (and Descent):** On the path up through the wooded Tiefentalgraben, then left and upwards across forested slopes. Move right into a small saddle with a small clearing and the Tiefental Forest Hut.
Through the forest in hair-pins to the foot of the rocks and right to the start of the Via Ferrata. On to a small shoulder and left on to steep rocks (uncomfortably exposed). Finally, straight up and over a small gap to the narrow summit.

*On the descent from the Ettaler Manndl.*

**An Additional Summit:** One can walk across to the Laber on a good path in ¾ hr. (good views and restaurant! – see Tour 3).

# 5  Schleierfälle und Scheibum

The Ammer gorge – a worthwhile visit

**Kammerl – Ammerleite – Schleierfälle – Kammerl – Scheibum**

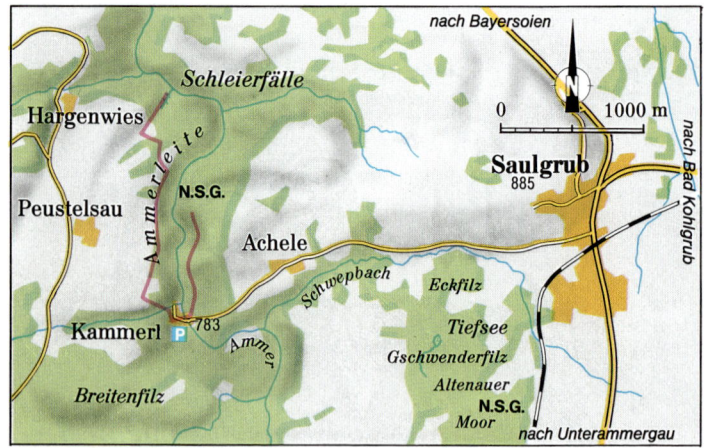

**Approach:** Saulgrub, 885 m., a holiday village near Bad Kohlgrub, beautifully situated with unspoiled views south.
**Start:** Car park at Kammerl, access from Saulgrub on a good, but narrow road, 3 km.
**Parking:** Car park before the bridge over the river Ammer.
**Walking Times:** Kammerl – Schleierfälle 45 min., return in similar time. Detour to Scheibum 15 min.
**Difficulty:** Good, well marked path with signs. No signing for Scheibum.
**Highest Point:** Ammerleite, 880 m.
**Refreshments:** None.
**Of Interest:** Schleierfälle, small waterfall formed from canopy-like limestone sedimentary deposits. Scheibum, where river Ammer has broken through the slanting layers of conglomerates and sandstone.

Between Oberammergau and Unterammergau the river Ammer flows as a gentle, pastoral stream through velvety, open meadows. Below Altenau, however, it vanishes in to a canyon which almost reaches the small community of Peißenberg. In the first part of the river there are two places of real natural interest. A gorge where the river has breached the layers of sandstone and conglomerate strata is known as Scheibum. A little farther downstream, moss-covered rocks tower above the river. Over these small tributary cascades – the Schleierfälle.

**From Kammerl to the Schleierfälle:** Across the Ammer bridge and steeply upwards to the open meadows at Peustelsau. From here north along the edge of the forest, always noting the signs. Then through open forest and across clearings to a forestry road joining from the left. Now the path leads right down a small valley and down a further step to the bank of the river Ammer. Right to the waterfalls.

**Detour to Scheibum:** From the car park on the (orog.) right bank of the river Ammer along a wide track through forest initially. Then on a footpath that avoids the outcrop to the right to Scheibum. Bathing possible.

*The river Ammer at the Scheibum breach.*

## 6  Hohe Bleick, 1638 m

A look-out high above the Wieskirche

**Unternogg – Saulochhütte – Anwurfhütte – Hohe Bleick – Niederbleick**

**Approach:** Altenau, 838 m, a solitary village in the meadows of the Ammer valley near Saulgrub.
**Start:** The road bridge over the river Halbammer, 500 m. W of Unternogg, which is equally 3 km. W of Altenau.
**Parking:** On the bridge.
**Walking Times:** Hohe Bleick 2½ hrs. Traverse to Niederbleick 20 min.
**Difficulty:** Almost half on a forestry road and footpaths without problems.
**Highest Point:** Hohe Bleick, 1638 m. Niederbleick, 1589 m.
**Refreshments:** None.
**Of Interest:** Bird's eye view from Niederbleick of the alpine fore-land.

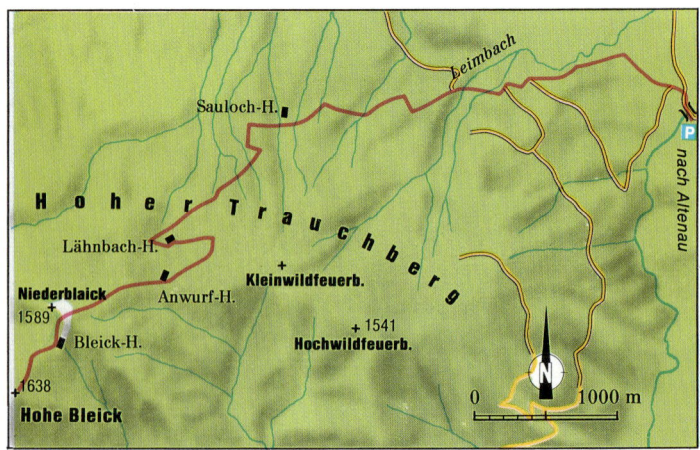

The Hohe Trauchberg is one of the largest, continuous tracts of forest in the region. The wide and high Bleick massif rises up out of the middle. It has two summits which only when both are climbed can it be called an ideal mountain view-point.
From the Hohe Bleick one looks across to the neighbouring Ammergauer alps and the Klammspitze, already a contrast with its harsh and alpine-like appearance. On the other hand, the Niederbleick, a grassy summit, thrusts north and one can enjoy the differing aspects of meadows, moor, forest, valley and hills.

**The Ascent (and Descent):** One walks north from the Halbammer bridge and after two minutes reaches a cross-roads. Here left and 500 m. farther on left again. At the third junction turn right. Further diagonally upwards through the forest to the Sauloch Hut, thence after a long curve to the Lähnbach Hut.

Now a smaller path for some distance left (E) and briefly through young trees. Then right diagonally upwards through open forest to the ridge. On the south side of the ridge to the Bleick Hut, an alpine hut, and left over a thinly wooded ridge to Hohe Bleick, or right across meadows to the nearby Niederbleick.

*On the way to Hohe Bleick.*

# 7 Steckenbergkreuz, Steckenberg, 1385 m

A lonely walk through woods and glades

**Unterammergau – Schleifmühlental – Steckenbergkreuz – Steckenberg – Kolbensattel – Schleifmühlental – Unterammergau**

**Approach:** Unterammergau, 836 m., village in the Ammer valley, situated 4 km. north of Oberammergau.
**Start:** At the mouth of the Schleifmühlental, 900 m., 1 km. SW of Unterammergau.
**Parking:** Large car park at the start.
**Walking Times:** Start – Steckenbergkreuz 1 hr., from there to Kolbensattel 1 hr.

**Difficulty:** Small but good path to Steckenbergkreuz, only a trodden track across the Steckenberg itself.
**Highest Point:** Either Steckenbergkreuz, 1220 m. or Steckenberg, 1385 m. (possibly Pürschlinghäuser, 1550 m.).
**Refreshments:** Kolbensattel Hut and the Pürschlinghäuser.

On the north ridge of the Steckenberg, high above Unterammergau stands a cross which is more than five meters high. Strangely enough from the valley it is rarely noticed although it is easy enough to see from below. A small, overgrown track leads up to this observation point.
The more ambitious can walk from there, over the Steckenberg on a path along the ridge, partly through open meadows, partly among towering spruce and finally younger trees to the Kolbensattel. It is a route for the genuine individualist and lover of peace and quiet. For, apart from one or two cows, he'll meet no other soul!

**To Steckenbergkreuz:** From the car park through the interesting Schleifmühlenklamm. Then on the forestry road to the valley junction. Follow the old track in the shallow gully to the left. After some ten minutes an equally old track leads almost vertically left out of the gully and upwards to a small glade. Along the left edge of the glade through young trees on an overgrown path almost directly to the cross.

**Over the Steckenberg to the Kolbensattel:** There is no proper route, however, one cannot lose the way if the ridge is followed (the fence is a reliable navigation aid!).
Upwards along the initially open ridge then in open forest to the highest point. On the other side, again in open forest descending across a second summit (sometimes swampy) and finally through young trees to the Kolbensattel.

**Possibilities for the Return Trip:**
a) As the traverse of the Steckenberg ends at the top station of the Kolbenlift,

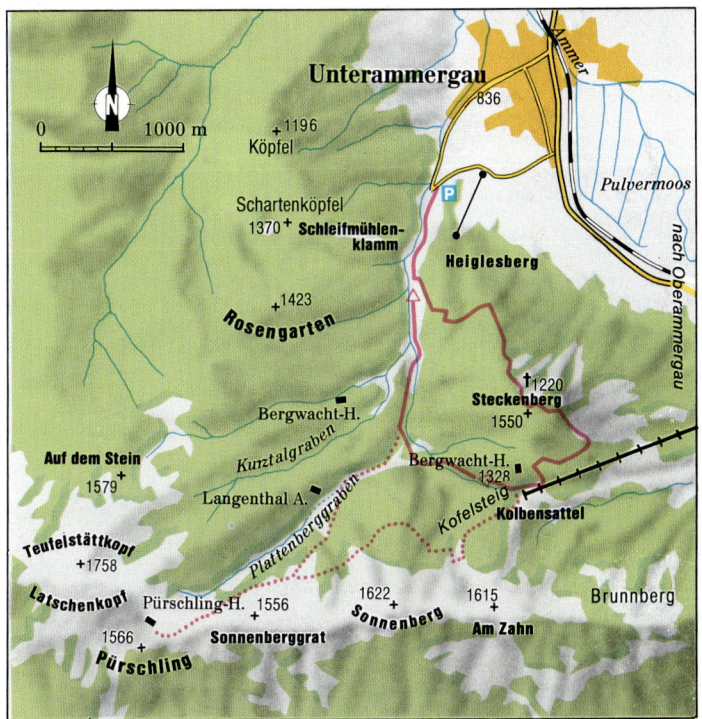

it is naturally the comfortable option to ride down to the valley. However, how to get back to the car? It would be only an hour's comfortable walk on a good path. The disadvantage is that the path runs alongside the heavily used main road.
b) Therefore it's worth – the by no means longer (in time) – westerly descent on foot. The start is hidden behind the top station. Down the rarely used path to the normal route to the Pürschlinghäuser and through the valley to the car park.
c) A longer walk to the Pürschling (see Tour 9).

# 8  Kofel, 1341 m

A flying visit to Oberammergau's popular landmark

**Oberammergau – Eastern ascent of the Kofel – Kofelsattel – Königssteig – Kolbensattel – Oberammergau**

**Approach:** Oberammergau, 837 m. Centre of the Ammer valley, famous for its Passion Play and wood carving, beautiful baroque church, murals on the walls of many houses.
**Start:** At the northern foot of the Döttenbühls. From Oberammergau on the road to Linderhof. Over the river Ammer and right at the foot of the mountain.
**Parking:** At the start of the climb.
**Walking Times:** To the summit 1¼ hrs. Descent via "Königsteig" and return to the car park, some 2¼ hrs.
**Difficulty:** A good path to the summit rocks. Then a few "pitches" secured by wire ropes but with no real difficulty.
**Highest Point:** Kofel, 1341 m.
**Refreshments:** Kolbenalm-Restaurant, 890 m.
**Of Interest:** Unique view down on to Oberammergau.

*Left: Kofel from the north-east.*

The Passion Play and wood carvers' village of Oberammergau lies in the broad meadowed basin of the Ammer valley. Only in the south does a mountain thrust its summit towards the outskirts of the village. This is the Kofel, a remarkable, audacious tooth of rock. Because of its somewhat prominent situation it appears to be more immense than its humble 1341 m. actually deserve.

However, a flying visit to this rocky pinnacle is truly rewarding and should not be avoided – unless one is put off by the few, wire rope secured, rocks at the top. The view on to Oberammergau is unique. Every tiny detail can be recognised – even with the naked eye.

**The Ascent:** From the car park through a small cleft on to a meadow. Cross this upwards to the edge of the forest and then on a good, but winding path up through the woods and outcrops to the Kofelsattel (shelter). Onwards right in a small gully through the boulder strewn forest. Now with the aid of a wire rope over the crag into a saddle then sometimes left of the edge (again wire ropes) up to the summit with its carved cross.

**Return via the "Königssteig":** Back to the Kofelsattel and to the start of the "Königssteig", a path which contours across the steep, gullied north slope of the Brunnberg. At the first fork sharp right and descend on a somewhat uneven track to the Kolbenalm (restaurant) which lies in a fine situation at the upper edge of the meadows.

Down a further 100 m. and either straight down to the centre of Oberammergau or right along the "Grottenweg" which traverses the slopes back to the car park.

## 9 Pürschling – Sonnenberg, 1622 m

A leisurely walk and an exciting ridge scramble

**Oberammergau – Kolbensattel – Pürschlinghäuser – Sonnenberggrat – Sonnenberg – Kolbenalm-Restaurant – Oberammergau**

**Approach:** Oberammergau, 837 m. Centre of the Ammer valley, famous for its Passion Play and wood carving, beautiful baroque church, murals on the walls of many houses.
**Start:** NW edge of the village of Oberammergau.
**Parking:** Large car park (Kolbenlift) in the Kolbengasse.
**Walking Times:** Kolbensattel – Pürschlinghäuser 1¼ hrs., Pürschling – Sonnenberg 1 hr.; descent 1¼ hrs.

**Difficulty:** Kolbensattel to Pürschling a comfortable mountain path. On the Sonnenberggrat a small track occasionally very steep.
**Highest Point:** Pürschlinghäuser, 1550 m., Sonnenberg, 1622 m.
**Refreshments:** Kolbensattel Hut, Pürschlinghäuser, Kolbenalm-Restaurant.
**Of Interest:** View down into Graswang valley (Linderhof), bizarre rock towers on the Sonnenberggrat.

*Left: On Sonnenberg.*

Driving south into the Ammer valley at Saulgrub one cannot avoid seeing a unique mountain ridge. Although appearing almost level it is broken-up by a number of small, grey rock pinnacles and towers. This is the ridge from Zahn to Sonnenberg, the goal of today's especially picturesque tour.
It consists of two utterly different experiences. The outward journey to the Pürschling belongs in the leisurely stroll category, the way back, along the Sonnenberggrat demands an experienced mountain walker. The narrow track winds around the afore mentioned pinnacles and in doing so traverses some remarkably precipitous ground.

**To the Pürschlinghäuser:** From the car park up the wide track to the lift, thence with the chair lift to the Kolbensattel, 1276 m. Opposite, about 20 m. higher and right on to a good, broad track contouring through woods and clearings to the west. Then somewhat steeper on a small road to the Pürschlinghäuser (DAV = German Alpine Club).

**Over the Sonnenberggrat and back to Oberammergau:** On the small road back to the nearest saddle in the ridge. Here a narrow footpath branches off. It rarely leads over the ridge, but snakes along the steep flanks and in and out of the rock towers and needles. Follow this path to just beyond the Sonnenberg summit which it traverses below and to the north. Detour on to the summit (magnificent views) up an earthy gully.
Soon the path drops down on to the northern slopes. Finally through open forest to the Kolbenalm-Restaurant and back to the car park.

## 10 Teufelstättkopf, 1758 m

The northern ascent – a special route to a well-known goal

**Unterammergau – Schleifmühlenklamm – Kühalm – Nordgrat – Teufelstättkopf – Pürschling – Unterammergau**

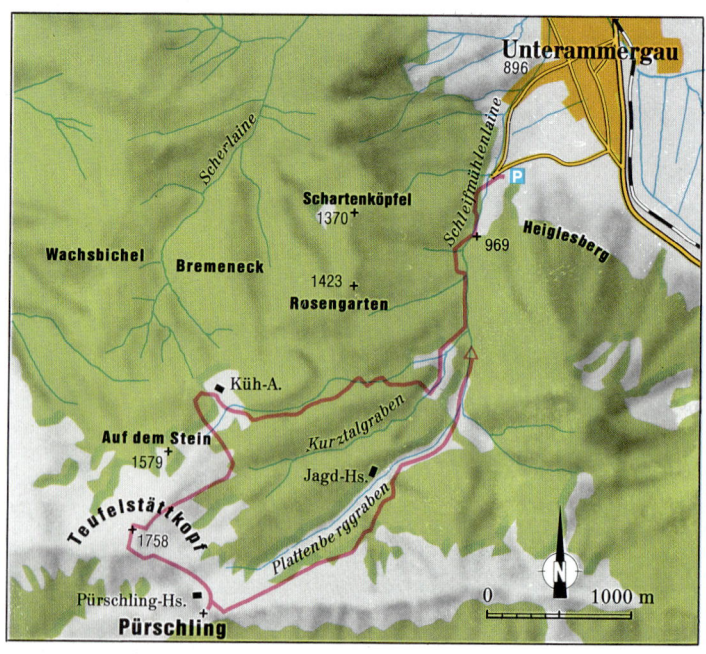

**Approach:** Unterammergau, 896 m., village in the Ammer valley, situated 4 km. N of Oberammergau.
**Start:** At the mouth of the Schleifmühlen valley, 900 m., 1 km. SW and above Unterammergau.
**Parking:** At the start.
**Walking Times:** Car park – Kühalm 1½ hrs., Kühalm – Teufelstättkopf 1¼ hrs. Descent to Pürschling ½ hr., descent to car park 1¼ hrs.
**Difficulty:** On the north ridge the route marking is somewhat sparse. No objective dangers.
**Highest Point:** Teufelstättkopf, 1758 m.
**Refreshments:** Pürschlinghäuser.
**Of Interest:** Schleifmühlenklamm, view down on to the Forggensee.

The Teufelstättkopf is one of the most interesting and striking mountains. It rises impressively above the surrounding tree-covered hills and is the first major peak of the Klammspitz ridge. The broad massif is defended virtually on all sides by steep, grassy slopes, while the numerous, small rocky ribs, pinnacles and outcrops provide decoration and a change of scenery. The summit itself perches like a rock hat on top of the massif.
Countless people approach over the ridge from the nearby Pürschling, while the northern route is hardly known. It is a proper route for individualists and for all those who bring a little mountain walking experience with them.

**The Ascent (northern route):** From the car park the most attractive way leads through the Schleifmühlenklamm. From there on a dusty forestry road to the meadows at 1200 m. At the junction right on the new road and on to Kühalm. Across the meadows to the ridge. At first in the forest and then in the open over varied countryside (numerous chamois) always near the ridge to the bristly, rocky summit massif. Finally, over a few harmless rocks to the summit cross.

**The Descent via the Pürschlinghäuser:** South on the well-worn track through rocky knolls then left over the grass ridge (narrow section) down to the Pürschlinghäuser. Down the small road into Langental and then on the forestry road or the old forest track to the car park.

*Teufelstättkopf and Pürschling seen from the south.*

## 11 Gießenbachtal

Lonely, original wooded valley

**From the Ettaler Sattel, over a salient in the east ridge of the Notkarspitze, into the valley and up the bed of the stream**

**Approach:** Ettal, 877 m. Popular goal for excursions, famous for the Benedictine Monastery and its lovely church, highest village in Ammer valley.
**Start:** Ettaler Sattel, 885 m., on the road to Oberau, 1 km. from Ettal.
**Parking:** Limited parking facilities at the junction with the forestry road at Ettaler Sattel.

**Walking Times:** Ettaler Sattel – Gießenbachtal 1¼ hrs. Return 1 hr.
**Difficulty:** Easy forestry road at first then a footpath in the stream bed, little climbing.
**Highest Point:** Mittleres Gießenbachtal, 1030 m.
**Refreshments:** None.
**Of Interest:** Ettaler Monastery.

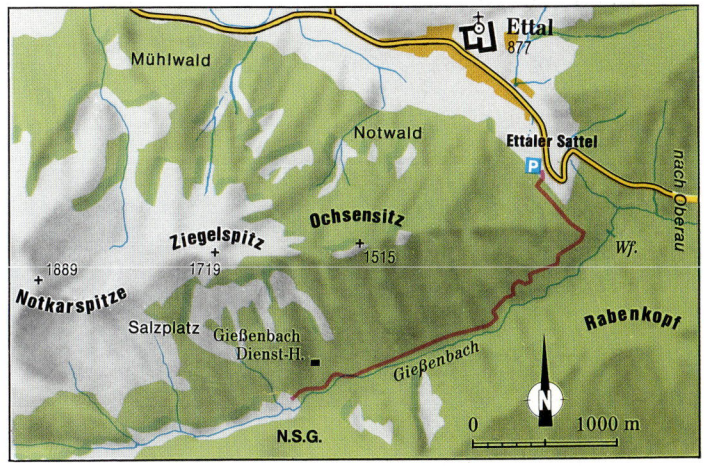

*Left: Gießenbachtal near Ettal.*

The Gießenbachtal cuts six kilometres deep into the Ammergauer alps, between the Notkarspitze and the Schafkopf. From Ettaler Berg nothing more than a deep, thickly wooded valley can be seen. Thus, no one is expecting such a fascinating mountain walk.
Its special attraction is the venture into increasingly primeval countryside. Initially, one is walking on a wide forestry road. Later this road narrows to a smaller track which gradually loses itself in the stream bed. Remaining are a few hardly discernible tracks and faint route marking. Simply follow the bed of the stream!

**From Ettaler Sattel into the Mittleres Gießenbachtal:** From the car park on the forestry road between two grassy knolls into a little, hidden valley. Here left in a longish climb to a spur on the east ridge of the Notkarspitze. Then contouring across the, sometimes, steep slopes one gradually approaches the picturesque, gorge-like depression of the Gießenbachtal.
On an ever narrowing path to its conclusion. Then following foot marks on the bed of the stream (especially exciting for children) several very photogenic spots are passed. Follow the valley until the track turns upwards to the left.
Return by the same route.

# 12 Notkarspitze, 1889 m

The mountain with one leisurely, scenic path and another which is steep and exciting

**Ettaler Sattel – Ochsensitz – Ziegelspitz – Notkarspitze – Notkar – Ettaler Mühle**

**Approach:** Ettal, 877 m., small village at the foot of the Laber, famous for the Benedictine monastery and its church.
**Start:** Ettaler Sattel, 885 m., on the road to Oberau, 1 km. from Ettal.
**Parking:** Limited parking facilities at the junction with the forestry road at Ettaler Sattel.
**Walking Times:** Ascent 3 hrs., descent 1½ hrs., possible return from Ettaler Mühle to Ettaler Sattel ½ hr.
**Difficulty:** Ascent on a good track. Descent in parts very steep – surefootedness is essential.
**Highest Point:** Notkarspitze, 1889 m.
**Refreshments:** None.
**Of Interest:** View of Kloster Ettal.

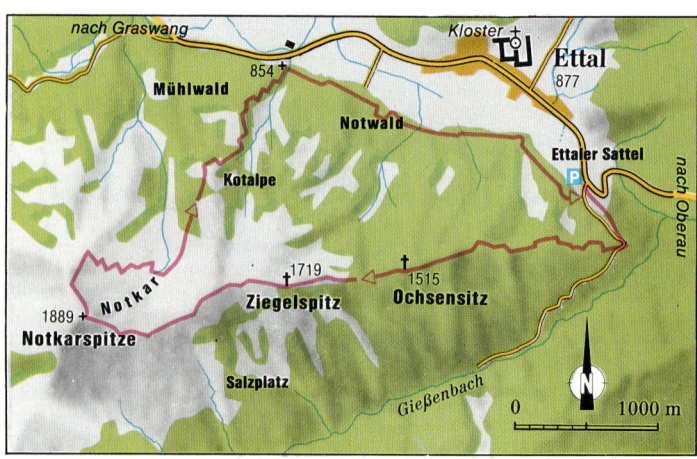

The Notkarspitze is a fine example of a lower alpine mountain, with steep, sometimes rocky wooded slopes in the lower regions and extensive areas of dwarf pine and open grass land on the upper flanks. There are almost uninterrupted views in all directions; naturally, most impressive are the near-by Wetterstein mountains.
A rather leisurely but somewhat lengthy trail leads over the east ridge, with fine views in its upper section. The route up the north slope is reserved for the more sporting with its, in parts extremely steep, rocky track. Both routes are

described as they are ideally suitable for a round-tour.

**Ascent over the east ridge:** From the saddle along the forestry road to the nearby east ridge. A footpath branches off. Keeping close to the ridge at first through thick woods, then increasingly in open country, below the Ochsensitz and over the top of the Ziegelspitz.

**Ascent from the Ettaler Mühle:** Up to the edge of the wood and a few metres to the right. The path starts here (sign). Very steeply up through the woods, then a long traverse across the dwarf pine tree covered slopes into the Notkar. Cross to the right on to the northern ridge, over it and up to the summit.

**From the Ettaler Mühle to Ettaler Sattel:** A path leads along the top edge of the meadows from the Ettaler Mühle to the Saddle.

*View from Oberammergau of the Notkarspitze.*

# 13 Ettaler Mühle – Linderhof

A valley tour with variations

**Ettaler Mühle – Sonnenweg – Graswang – Linderhof and back on the other side of the valley; possible extension of the tour as far as Oberammergau**

**Approach:** Ettal, 877 m., popular village for excursions, famous for the Benedictine monastery and its church. The highest village in the Ammer valley.
**Start:** Ettaler Mühle, 840 m., a restaurant on the road to Graswang, 1.5 km. from Ettal.
**Parking:** At the Ettaler Mühle.
**Walking Times:** Ettaler Mühle – Graswang ¾ hr., farther to Linderhof 1 hr. Return in similar time. Detour via Oberammergau a further 1 hr.
**Difficulty:** Forestry roads and easy paths.
**Highest Point:** Upper edge of the castle gardens at Linderhof, 1010 m.
**Refreshments:** Restaurants and cafés at Graswang and Linderhof.
**Of Interest:** Linderhof castle, which was built as a country seat for the Bavarian King Ludwig II.

Between Oberammergau, Ettal and Linderhof the upper Ammer valley is wide and consists in parts of marshy meadows and in others of open forest. On both sides of the valley footpaths and forestry roads inter-connect to form abundant walking circuits.

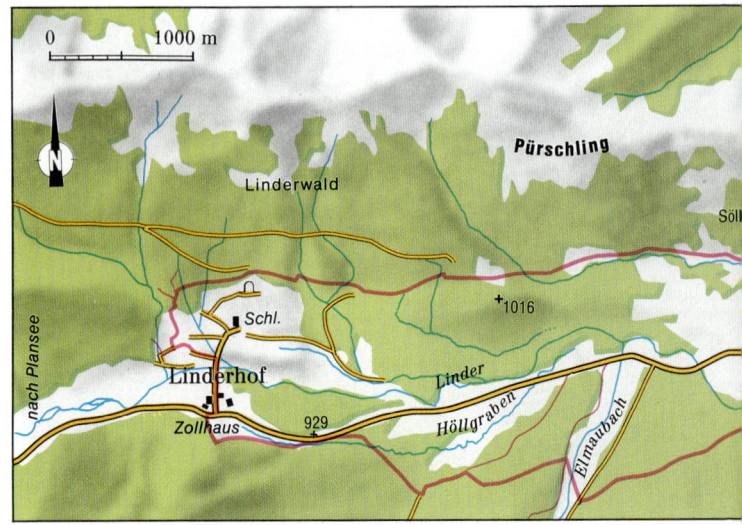

**The Route on the North of the Valley:** From the Ettaler Mühle through the meadows (wonderful marsh vegetation) and straight across the valley to the foot of the mountains in the north. Here the footpath from Oberammergau joins.
Along this track on the edge of the meadows to Graswang. Keep the village left and on to a forestry road. Follow this road through woods and glades, gradually climbing to the fence surrounding the Linderhof gardens. Through a gate and downhill to the castle.

**The Route on the South of the Valley:** From Linderhof south, across the river Linder and the main road. At first on a footpath and then on a forestry road east through open forest always following the signs and the "blue-white-blue" markers.
Over the dry Elmaugriess (bed of the stream), through woods and meadows almost to Graswang. Without crossing the bridge continue to Dickelschwaig and the edge of the forest and on to Ettaler Mühle.

**Oberammergau Loop:** Remain on the bank of the Ammer until reaching the S edge of Oberammergau. Left over the bridge and along the path parallel to the road until meeting the "out" track described initially.

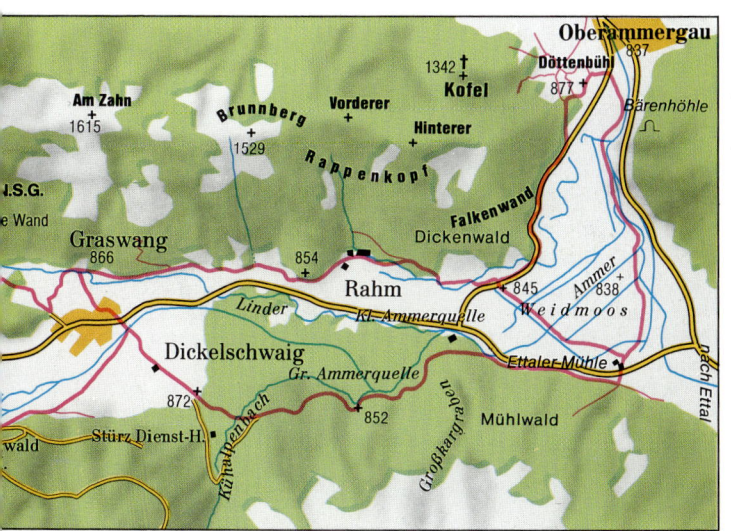

# 14 Kuhalpenbachtal

Exploring a long, interesting mountain stream

**Graswang – Dickelschwaig – Kuhalpenbachtal – Kuhalm – Schattenwald – Graswang**

*Right: Waterfall in the Brünstelgraben (Kuhalpenbachtal).*

**Approach:** Graswang, 866 m., small village in the wide, meadowed valley of the river Linder between Oberammergau and Linderhof.
**Start:** Eastern edge of the village at the junction of the sandy road to Dickelschwaig.
**Parking:** Limited parking at the junction.
**Walking Times:** To Kuhalm 2 hrs. Back on the forestry road 1½ hrs.
**Difficulty:** A small but adequate path through a gorge-like valley, very steep in parts.
**Highest Point:** Kuhalm, 1326 m.
**Refreshments:** None.
**Of Interest:** Beautiful rocky gorge, several waterfalls, cascading ledges.

Many of the mountain streams in the Ammergauer alps confluence with their main valleys over rocky steps and ledges. All of them are picturesque with steep walls, rocky chasms and ledges, waterfalls and rock pools. However, to the chagrin of lovers of primeval streams, most of them are inaccessible!

An exception, however, is the Kuhalpenbachtal, which emerges at Graswang. A small path provides access to this gully along its entire length. In the lower reaches it remains as nature intended. The upper stretch has been transformed artificially to a series of steps and the resultant cascades. From the Kuhalm one can walk back, either the same way or, more leisurely, on the forestry road.

**Through the Kuhalpenbachtal to the Kuhalm:** From the junction along the sandy road to the forestry buildings at Dickelschwaig and past them on to the edge of the forest. At the junction right then down into the, at this stage, wide stream bed. Before the gorge up on to the right (orog.) bank and climb above the rift. Now opposite are the waterfalls of the Sesselgraben and Brünstelsgraben.

The upper part of the valley has been "stepped" and is reminiscent of the small, artificial waterfalls in parks or gardens. Finally, over the last ledge to the Kuhalm.

**Back along the Forestry Road:** From the Kuhalm on the road north, mainly through open forest and across several deep gullies. Remain on the road until the valley has been reached. Right at the junction then parallel to the river Linder back to Graswang and the start.

**Option of a Mountain Walk:** From the Kuhalm east and follow the road to its end. Cross the following slopes on a footpath into a wide saddle and finally, by means of its south-west ridge on to the Notkarspitze, with its fine views (see Tour 12, about 2½ hrs. from the Kuhalm).

# 15 Around the Brunnenkopf

Belvedere, rocky summit and panorama trail

**Linderhof – Reitweg – Brunnenkopfhäuser – Klammspitze and back. Alternatively a high mountain trail to the Pürschling, descent to Linderhof**

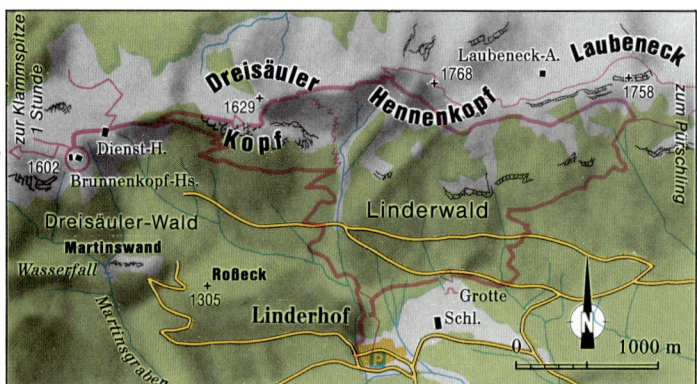

**Approach:** Linderhof, 942 m., in the wooded Linder valley. Castle of Ludwig II, the Bavarian King.
**Start:** At Linderhof itself.
**Parking:** Large, fee-paying car park at Linderhof.
**Walking Times:** Linderhof – Brunnenkopfhäuser 2 hrs. From there to Klammspitze 1½ hrs. Detour to the Brunnenkopf 20 mins. high mountain trail to Pürschling 2 hrs.
**Difficulty:** To the Brunnenkopfhäuser, a gentle walk, to the Klammspitze steep and surefootedness essential. The high-level route to Pürschling, a well-prepared path which leads, however, across some very steep ground.
**Highest Point:** Brunnenkopf, 1710 m., poss. Große Klammspitze, 1925 m., Pürschlinghäuser, 1550 m.
**Refreshments:** Brunnenkopfhäuser and Pürschlinghäuser.
**Of Interest:** Schloß Linderhof, impressive rocky scenery on the Klammspitze. The high mountain trail to Pürschling.

Some walkers, who have climbed to the Brunnenkopf from Linderhof, the world-famous castle of the "fairytale King" Ludwig II., will not have been satisfied with their day's work!
There are two opportunities for them to do something really worthwhile. Those with mountaineering experience will climb the Klammspitze, an elegant rock peak rising high above its surroundings. The less ambitious will choose the well-prepared high mountain trail to the Pürschling. This is a

unique panorama trail which remains between 1500 m. and 1600 m. as it contours across the southern slopes of the Klammspitze ridge.

**From Linderhof to Brunnenkopf:** The wide path to the Brunnenkopfhäuser starts left, behind the hotel. For much of the way it remains in the forest, emerging into the open only just before the ridge. From the hut a short climb to the nearby Brunnenkopf summit.

**On the Große Klammspitze:** On a mountain path across the steep, grassy slopes of the Brunnenkopf into a cirque at the foot of the Klammspitze. Then left through a small saddle in the ridge and up very steep rugged terrain to the summit. Return the same way.

**High mountrain trail to the Pürschling and Descent to Linderhof:** From the Brunnenkopfhäuser back in the direction of Linderhof for about 10 mins. At the track junction left. The path to Pürschling cannot be missed. It is not necessary to walk all the way to the Pürschling. At the foot of the Teufelstättkopf, a well trodden track branches off sharply right and down steeply to Linderhof. On this track back to the car park.

*The Klammspitze in evening mood.*

# 16 Around the Hasental

A silent walk through an unusual mountain feature

**Lindergrieß – Sägertal – Bäckenalmsattel – Hanging Valley – Hasentalkopf – Lösertaljoch – Sägertal – Lindergrieß**

**Approach:** Linderhof, 942 m., in the richly wooded Linder valley. Castle of the Bavarian king Ludwig II.
**Start:** Bridge over the river Linder, 970 m., 2 km. west of the Customs Post at Linderhof.
**Parking:** Large car park at the roadside.
**Walking Times:** Linderbrücke – Bäckenalmsattel 2¼ hrs., Bäckenalmsattel – Hanging Valley – Lösertaljoch 1 hr. Detour to the Hasentalkopf 20 mins. Return from Lösertaljoch 1¾ hrs.
**Difficulty:** In parts narrow but always good paths.
**Highest Point:** Scheinbergjoch, 1764 m., poss. Hasentalkopf, 1797 m.
**Refreshments:** None.
**Of Interest:** Hanging Valley with small lake. Vertical rock slip on the Hasentalkopf. View of the Ammergauer "Matterhorn" – Geiselstein.

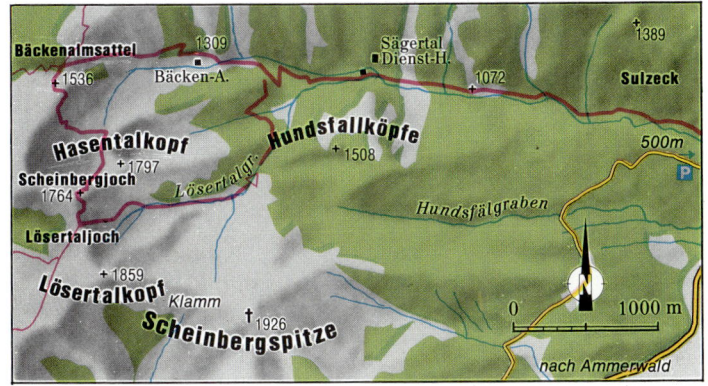

Left: In the Bäckenalmsattel with the Hochplatte in the background.

Between the Klammspitze ridge and the Hochplatte range lies a small, solitary massif which most walkers hardly notice. It is formed by the Vorderer Scheinberg and Hasentalkopf. There should be no confusion with the Scheinbergspitze (see Tour 17). The Hasental massif presents a quite special mountain feature. Hidden beneath the horseshoe-like summit ridge is a small cirque (basin-shaped valley). The valley floor lies some 60 m. lower than its rim at the lowest point where one can find a tiny lake which appears to have no form of natural drainage.

**The Route to the Basin-shaped Valley:** From the car park across the Linder bridge and through the thickly wooded Sägertal to the end of the forestry road. Further on a forest track then a footpath westwards on to the Bäkkenalmsattel. Here left and winding up across a steep, overgrown slope on to a shoulder. A slight descent to the rim of the basin. Around the left flank of the "funnel" and diagonally up to the Scheinbergjoch, 1764 m.

**Hasentalkopf:** From the saddle (Scheinbergjoch) mainly left just below the rocky ridge on a small path in 15 mins. to the attractive summit.

**Descent through the Lösertal:** From the Scheinbergjoch across a steep slope down into the nearby Lösertaljoch. Then turning left down the Lösertal to the Lösertalmösel. Traverse the now wooded slopes north through a steep gully (Hasentalgraben) and across to the route in, just below Bäkkenalmsattel.

# 17 Scheinbergspitze, 1926 m

A peaceful tour to a beautiful, solitary pyramid

**Neualmgrieß – South Ridge – Scheinbergspitze**

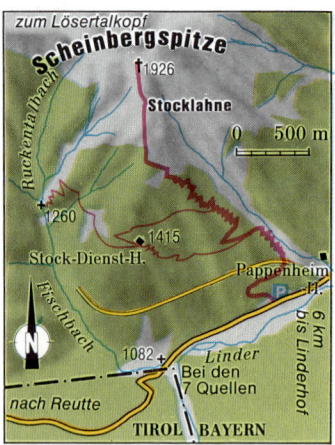

**Approach:** Linderhof, 942 m., in the wooded valley of the river Linder. Famous castle of the Bavarian King Ludwig II.
**Start:** Neualmgrieß, at the junction of the main road with a forestry road right, 1 km. before the border (not the Customs Post!).
**Parking:** Car park right on the junction with the forestry road.
**Walking Time:** 2½ hrs.
**Difficulty:** Narrow but good path, only in the last few metres to the summit is it somewhat rocky.
**Highest Point:** Scheinbergspitze, 1926 m.
**Refreshments:** None.
**Of Interest:** Views of the north faces of the Kuchelberg, Kreuzspitze and Geierköpfe.

A beautiful, dark and solitary pyramid reaching high above the Graswang valley, can be seen already from as far away as the road between Ettal and Oberammergau. It is the Scheinbergspitze, the eastern-most outpost of the Hochplatte range. A mountain, with forests, open meadows and dwarf pine and boasting a small rock face at its summit. However, compared to many of the other mountains in the Ammergauer alps, it is rarely climbed. Yet, the track up from the south offers an ascent of no difficulty. Its open forest and the many glades present uninterrupted views on to the impressive northern faces of the Kuchelberg, Kreuzspitze, 2185 m, and the Geierköpfe.

**The Ascent:** On the forestry road to the second bend. Here, at the edge of the Stockgraben (ditch) a path breaks off to the north (¼ hr. – signpost). At first parallel to the aforementioned ditch, later steeply left and upwards through open forest. Then across glades and woods on to the wide, dwarf pine covered south ridge to a false summit, a few meters down and up the rocky slope to the cross.
Warning! The attractive-looking traverse to the Lösertaljoch is not to be recommended.

*The Scheinbergspitze, the ascent ridge is left.*

The connecting ridge is overgrown by an almost impenetrable jungle of dwarf pines.

# 18 Krähe, 2012 m

Long and unusually fascinating circuit

**Ammerwald – Roggental – Roggentalgabel – Fensterl – Krähe – Gabelschrofensattel – Straußbergsattel – Schützensteig – Ammerwald**

**Approach:** Hotel "Ammerwald", 1080 m., in a clearing in the Ammerwald. Access via Linderhof or Reutte (A) via the Plansee.
**Start:** Hotel "Ammerwald"
**Parking:** At Hotel "Ammerwald"
**Walking Times:** Ammerwald – Roggental – Krähe 3 hrs. Descent over the Straußbergsattel 2½ hrs.

**Difficulty:** Without difficulty, however, in parts a narrow track on steep ground.
**Highest Point:** Krähe, 2012 m., poss. Hochplatte, 2082 m.
**Refreshments:** Only in Hotel "Ammerwald".
**Of Interest:** Mountain streams (Roggental), large rock window, Krähenhöhle and savage, rocky scenery.

*On the way to the Weitalpspitze.*

The Krähe, situated W of the mighty Hochplatte, 2082 m., is a mountain with countless possibilities. Here the walker can put together his (or her!) own route based on individual experience, ability and mood. We have described the most interesting circuit, briefly mentioning the other alternatives. The trips offer an abundance of impressions and surprises. Among them are "Fensterl" (little window), a huge rock door and path right through the ridge, as well as the vertical north face of the Krähe.

**Through the Roggental and up Krähe:** From the hotel some 400 m. on the road north and then left on a forestry track to the confluence of the Roggentalbach. Follow the stream bed until the valley forks. Left through a small cirque on the Roggentalgabel. Diagonally across the steep, grassy slopes to the "Fensterl" and then walking south of the ridge on the Krähe.

**Across the Straußbergsattel back into the Ammertal:** From Krähe briefly along the ridge west in a shallow gully. Then through a gap between the rock walls to the north and steeply down passing the Krähenhöhle (cave). In the nearby Gabelschrofensattel is a small but impressive hole through the rock wall. Now west and down into the Schwangauer Kessel. Halfway down the slope turn south onto the bordering ridge and beyond it in wide curves (former bridle path) on to the Straußbergsattel. Now south and almost level into a saddle, 1431 m., and down the "Schützensteig" to the hotel.

**Alternative Routes:** From the "Fensterl" an ascent of the Hochplatte – ½ hr. Rocky and in parts secured by a wire rope; only for the more experienced. – Or, from the Roggentalgabel a descent through the Köhlebachtal to the saddle, 1431 m. (the shortest possible alternative). – Or, from the Roggentalgabel via a small track (surefootedness required) south on to the summit of the Hochblasse, 1988 m. – ¼ hr.

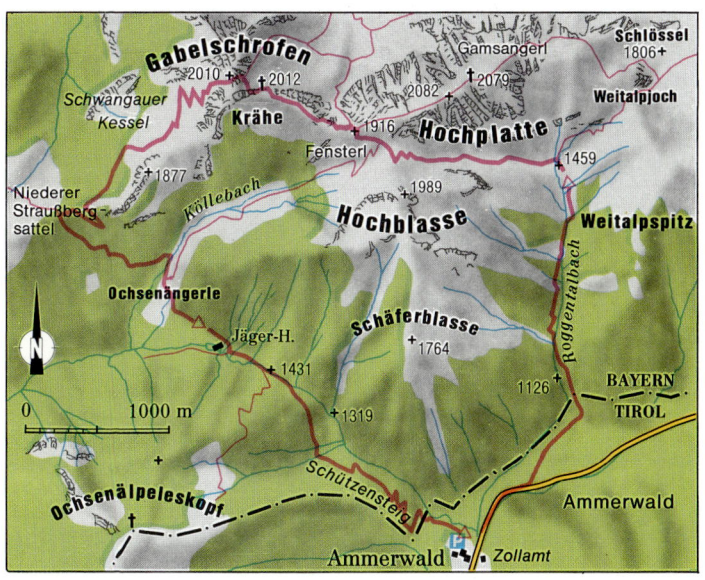

# 19 Westlicher Geierkopf, 2143 m

An impressive mountain between the Ammerwald and the Plansee

**Erzbachtal – Teufelstal – Zwergenbergalm – South Ridge – Westl. Geierkopf**

**Approach:** Hotel "Ammerwald", 1080 m., in a clearing, utterly isolated in the Ammerwald. Access via Linderhof or Reutte (A) via Plansee.
**Start:** 2 km. south of the hotel on the road to the Plansee. At the bridge over the Teufelstalbach, 1030 m.
**Parking:** On the left side of the road before the bridge.
**Walking Time:** 3½ hrs.
**Difficulty:** Small, but good path. Near the summit steep and rocky.
**Highest Point:** West summit of the Geierköpfe, 2143 m.
**Refreshments:** None.
**Of Interest:** Fine view of the Plansee.

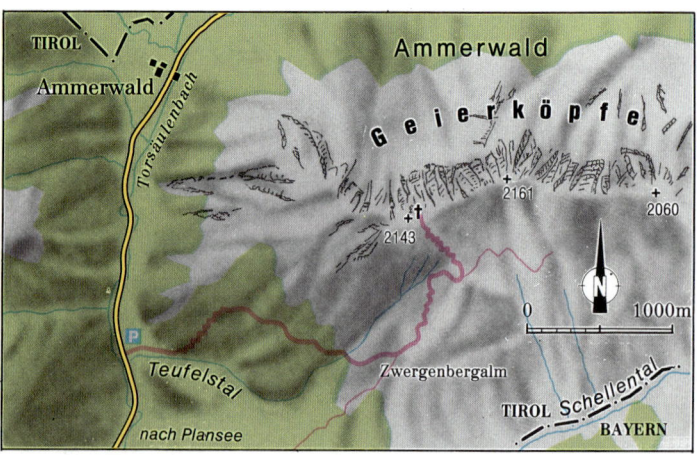

Anyone using the road through the Ammerwald from Linderhof to the Plansee cannot but admire the 3 km. wide northern face of the Geierköpfe. It is the most impressive sight in the whole of the Ammergauer alps!
The long ridge culminates in three summits. The middle one is the highest and being the most difficult (rock climbing Grade I – Moderate), not an objective for the pure mountain walker. He will be content with the West Summit, which is almost as high and to which there is a path; and although the summit is somewhat steep and strenuous it presents no major difficulties. The tour of the Geierkopf leaves an especially strong impression of an entirely unspoiled, primeval landscape.

**The Ascent:** The track begins north of the Teufelstal stream at a signpost. After a climb of almost 400 m. up and across the steep slopes above the main valley, the track turns towards the east, crossing a series of steeply cut stream gullies. At the Zwergenbergalm a path turns north, through trees and dwarf pines on to the southern spur of our chosen summit. Then, partly on the ridge, partly on the left of it steeply up to the summit.

*View of the Plansee from the Geierköpfe.*

# 20 Neuweidtal

A lonely walk in a primeval mountain cirque

**Plansee – Neuweidtal – Hebertal and back**

**Approach:** Linderhof, 942 m., in the wooded valley of the river Linder. Famous castle, which was built as a country seat for the Bavarian King Ludwig II.
**Start:** NE bank of the Plansee, 976 m. From Linderhof on the Ammerwald road (border) to the N bank of the lake (Hotel "Forelle"), at junction turn east.
**Parking:** Large car park on the edge of the lake.

**Walking Times:** Outward 1 hr. Back only a little less.
**Difficulty:** Forestry roads.
**Highest Point:** Confluence of the Hebertal, 1050 m.
**Refreshments:** None en route, otherwise Hotel "Forelle".
**Of Interest:** Plansee, second largest lake in the Tyrol, fjord-like nestling between steep mountains. Almost no development.

This comfortable, pleasant walk follows a valley below the unspoiled, towering mountains. At the end of the road all traces of civilisation vanish! Here only nature has influenced the countryside and that, in a unique way.
The almost 1000 m. high north-east flank of the Plattberg is not a compact, firm face compared to those that are to be found in the Wetterstein. The friable and rotten rock suffers particularly from the weather. This results in

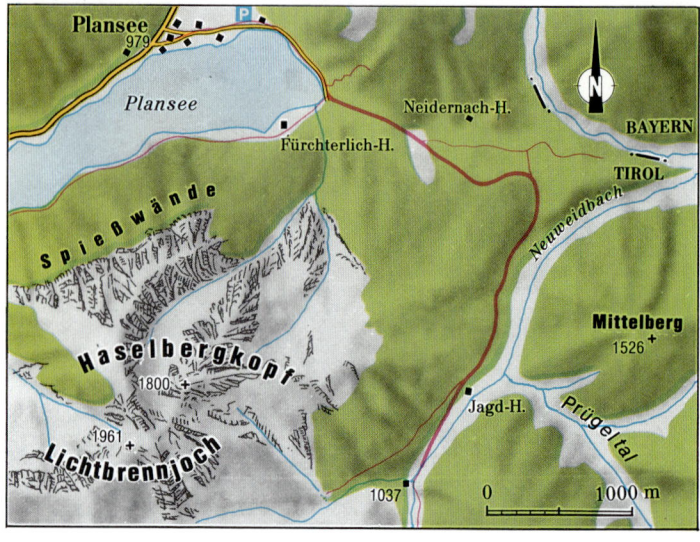

*View of the Plattberg.*

bizarre natural features; the rock walls scarred by deep gullies and stream beds filled with boulders and scree.

**From Plansee into the Neuweidtal:** From the car park to the eastern tip of the lake and then on the wide sandy road to the east until after a meadow a narrower road branches right. On this road and at the next junction left into the forest. Past a hut and follow a long curve to the banks of the Neuweidbach, which flows through a gorge at this point.
Climbing briefly to the next junction, then left into the steeply sided valley. At a small clearing the road crosses a boulder-filled bed of a stream. A few minutes later the valley fork (left the Hebertal and right the Pitzental). Return along the same route.

# 21 Stepbergalm or Kramer

Vis-a-vis with the Zugspitze

**Garmisch – Kammerleine Valley – Stepbergalm – poss. Kramersteig – Kramerspitz – Fürstenbrunnen – St. Martin – Garmisch**

**Approach:** Garmisch-Partenkirchen, 708 m., holiday and winter sports village in the wide basin of the Loisach with magnificent mountain backdrop.
**Start:** Maximilianshöhe, 850 m. Branch off at the Tierheim (Dogs' Home). Reached via the Griesen road (Fernpass). At the traffic lights opposite the barracks (USA), right over the river Loisach then left and up into the forest.
**Parking:** At the side of the road.

**Walking Times:** Garmisch – Stepbergalm 2¼ hrs., Stepbergalm – Kramerspitz 1½ hrs.
**Difficulty:** Good, but rocky paths to the Stepbergalm. Near the summit steeper and a little exposed. No real difficulty.
**Highest Point:** Stepbergalm, 1583 m., Kramerspitz, 1985 m.
**Refreshments:** Stepbergalm, poss. St. Martin-Restaurant.
**Of Interest:** Uninterrupted view of the Wetterstein.

A quarter of Garmisch-Partenkirchen's mountain background is occupied by one, single mountain, the Kramer, 1985 m. The description "mountain" is somewhat misleading. The Kramer is an entire massif, rising steeply, broad and imposing with a remarkably dark hue. The conifers produce this colouring; spruces on the lower slopes and higher, the dwarf pines cover the mountain completely. Only a few pale grey outcrops provide some lighter relief. The walk to the Kramer summit is relatively long. Hence, many only climb up into the meadowy basin of the Stepbergalm. Even this offers magnificent views of the Wetterstein with its towering rock faces; an ever-present showpiece on all of Kramer's paths.

**To the Stepbergalm:** From the Dogs' Home (Tierheim) left about 1 km. through the Military Training Area, then right up into the forest. At first a wide but soon narrower track (well signed) west into the valley of the Kammerleine. Remaining high above the stream upwards to the meadows around the Stepbergalm, crossing two deep gullies towards the top.

**From the Stepbergalm to the Kramerspitz:** East across the meadows to the ridge, then up through an alley of dwarf pine and south beneath the ridge to just below the summit. An outcrop is avoided low down to the south. A ramp leads to the summit cross.

**Direct Descent:** North to a nearby grassy saddle, then on the path through sometimes extremely rocky ground. Avoid a rock tower low down to the north and on along the ridge over several more rocky knolls into the lowest saddle. From the eastern end of the saddle down south on to a wider track. Down this, past a Belvedere built in the rock wall, to the restaurant at St. Martin and further on to the "Kramerplateauweg". On this, right and back to the car park.

*Left: On the way to the Stepbergalm.*

## 22 Bichlbacher und Tuftlalm

A panorama route beneath the Daniel

**Lermoos – Lähn – Bichlbacher Alm – Grüner Ups – Tuftlalm, poss. Daniel**

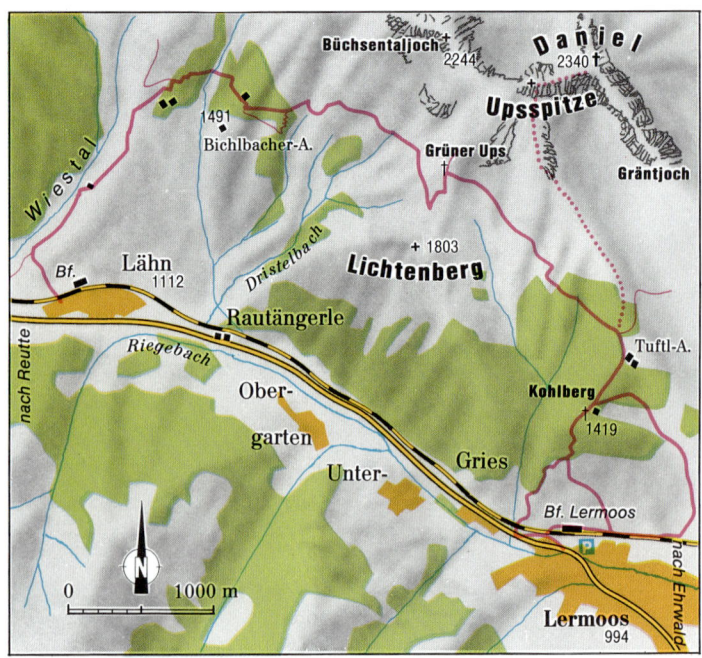

**Approach:** Lermoos, 994 m., holiday village in the Ehrwald basin at the foot of the Grubigstein with fine views of the Wetterstein und Mieminger mountains.

**Start:** Lähn, 1112 m. Village 5 km. from Lermoos on the line to Reutte. Reached either by train or walking on the Zugspitz-Panorama Trail above the valley to the north. About 1¼ hrs.

**Parking:** In the Danielstraße near the station.

**Walking Times:** Lähn – Bichlbacher Alm 1½ hrs., Bichlbacher Alm – Ups – Tuftlalm 1½ hrs. Descent ¾ hr. Lermoos – Tuftlalm 1½ hrs., Tuftlalm – Daniel 2 hrs.

**Difficulty:** 'Panorama Trail' – in parts narrow paths without problems. Daniel ascent requires surefootedness.

**Highest Point:** Bichlbacher Alm, 1491 m; Grüner Ups, 1852 m.; poss. Daniel, 2340 m.

**Refreshments:** Tuftlalm.

**Of Interest:** Views into the Ehrwald basin and of the Zugspitze.

*Daniel – seen from the vicinity of Garmisch.*

Daniel's slopes rise steeply over Lermoos, a massive flank some 1300 m. high. Yet in these slopes are hidden small shoulders and clearings which afford room for pasture and meadow. There are two summits, too, which jut out above the valley. The countryside is ideal for a panorama route. It is traversed from west to east – only then can the Zugspitze and the Mieminger mountains be continuously in view. Nevertheless, Daniel will be what attracts the mountaineer.

**The Circuit via Grüner Ups:** Out of Lähn station and west over the tracks and on to a road diagonally left. Then curving right over meadows upwards for about an hour. After the junction straight across the slopes to the right (just below the Bichlbacher Alm) and over several gullies on to the open shoulder of the Lichtenberg, 1803 m. Then briefly up and left to Grüner Ups. Diagonally down across the slopes to the Tuftlalm and back to Lermoos station.

**To Daniel:** From the swimming pool at Lermoos on small roads and footpaths to the Tuftlalm (refreshments!). Through woods, later among dwarf pines and upwards steeply along a rocky spur towards the Upsspitze. Some 100 m. below the summit right along the connecting ridge and up Daniel (surefootedness needed).

# 23 Pleisspitze, 2225 m

A mountain walk over a grass covered summit

**Top station of the Grubig Lift – Wolfratshauser Hütte – Gartnertal – Sommerbergjöchl – Pleisspitze – Gartnertal – Untergarten – Lermoos**

*Spring Gentian.*

**Approach:** Lermoos, 994 m., holiday village in the Ehrwald basin at the foot of the Grubigstein with fine views of the Wetterstein und Mieminger mountains.
**Start:** Top station of the Grubig cable car, 2020 m.
**Parking:** At the bottom station.
**Walking Times:** Descent from the lift into Gartnertal ¾ hr. Ascent from there to the Pleisspitze 2½ hrs. Complete descent to Lermoos about 2 hrs.
**Difficulty:** Small paths in partly steep ground.
**Highest Point:** Top station, 2020 m., Pleisspitze 2225 m.
**Refreshments:** Grubigsteinhaus, Wolfratshauser Hut (both at the start of the tour!).
**Of Interest:** North face of the Gartnerwand, rich vegetation.

The Pleisspitze is nothing short of a "Teaching Trail" for would-be geologists. Above it are the precipitous, 500 m. high, northern slopes of the Gartnerwand, 2377 m. They consist of layers of the friable, dolomitic limestone. The slopes of the Pleisspitze present an unusual contrast for they are overgrown entirely by grass – even on the steepest parts. This too, is a result of the geology where here, the different sedimentary strata has broken down by weathering. So much so that a fertile top soil is the result; which, in turn is responsible for an abundance of wild flowers.

**From Grubigsteinhaus to Pleisspitze:** On a good track north down to the nearby Wolfratshauser Hut then on a smaller path westwards across steep slopes down into the Gartnertal, 1500 m. Over the stream to a track junction. Keeping right (orog.) above the deep gully and up the valley on a wide ledge. Then through a steep cutting into the Sommerbergjöchle, 2001 m. Along the grass ridge and over a false top to the summit.

**Direct Descent to Lermoos:** Back to the track junction in Gartnertal. In the deep stream bed descending quickly to about 100 m. above the main valley. Now right on a small road out of the valley on to the open pastures of Untergarten. Above Gries and back to Lermoos.

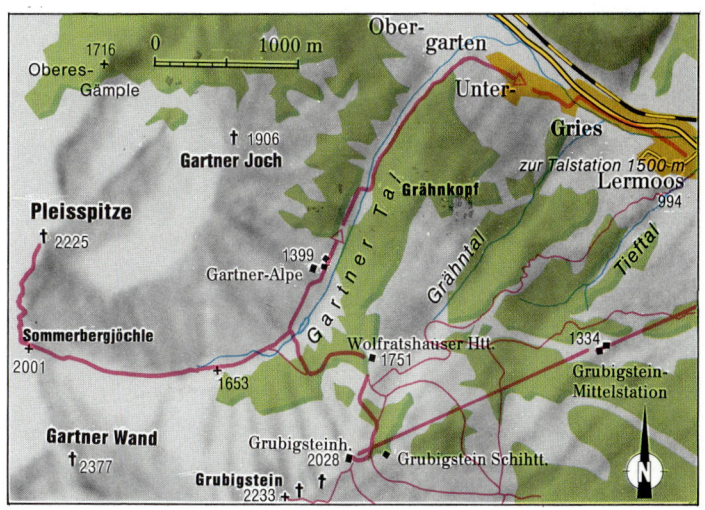

# 24 Grubig-Fernpass-Circuit

A descent from Grubig to the lakes on the Fernpass

**Top Station of the Grubig Lift – (Grubigstein) – Grubig – Fernpass – Blindsee – Loisachquellen – Biberwier – Wachtersteig – Lermoos**

**Approach:** Lermoos, 994 m., holiday village in the Ehrwald basin at the foot of the Grubigstein with fine views of the Wetterstein und Mieminger mountains.
**Start:** Top station of the Grubigstein cable car, 2020 m.
**Parking:** At the bottom station.
**Walking Times:** Top station – Fernpass 2 hrs., Fernpass – Biberwier 1½ hrs., Biberwier – Lermoos ¾ hr., poss. detour up the Grubigstein ¾ hr.

**Difficulty:** Small, but good mountain paths. The ascent of the Grubigstein is steep and requires surefootedness.
**Highest Point:** Top station of the Grubigstein chairlift, 2020 m., poss. Grubigstein, 2233 m.
**Refreshments:** Grubigsteinhaus, Zugspitzblick-Restaurant, cafés and restaurants in Biberwier.
**Of Interest:** The lakes which decorate the prehistoric rock falls north of the Fernpass.

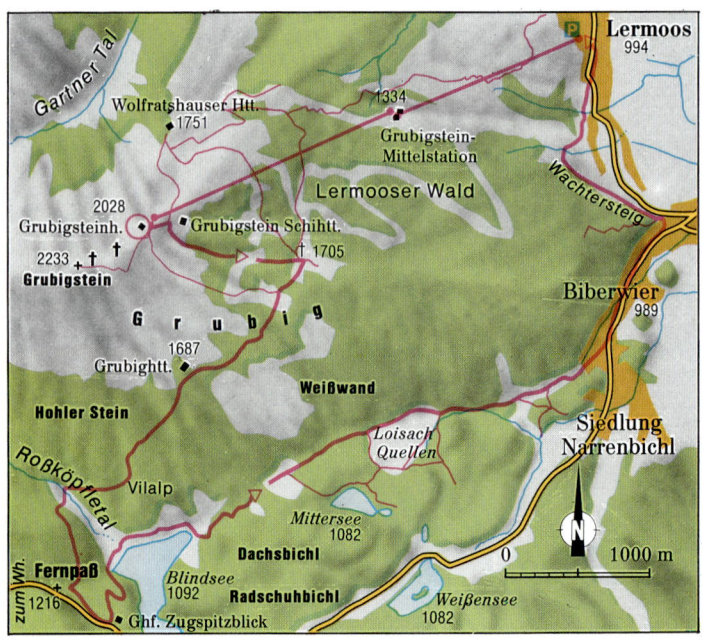

68

*Fernsteinsee, south of the Fernpass.*

Today, for a change we offer a mountain tour in reverse – that is , a walk from the tops down! What are chairlifts for anyway? So we start today with the height and the views. Especially appealing is the view down into the Ehrwald basin. Later in the walk the attraction is the countryside around the Fernpass. Here, after the Ice Age, massive rock falls plunged into the valley and created a unique landscape of small knolls, valleys and lakes.

**From Grubigsteinhaus to the Fernpass:** From the top station east down undulating ground for about ¼ hr (in direction of the Sonnenspitze). The track then bends sharp right and leads diagonally down across steep slopes into the steeply eroded valley of the Roßköpfltal. Cross the gully and through the forest to the northern end of the Fernpass. A few minutes right to the Fernpass-Hotel – left for the Zugspitzblick-Restaurant.

**From the Fernpass to Lermoos:** At the Zugspitzblick-Restaurant the path leads off and along the steep, rocky north bank of the Blindsee and down to the meadows where the river Loisach has its source. Past Narrenbichl hamlet and on to Biberwier. Through the village to just below the church. Now left and briefly up on to a low ridge and back to Lermoos along the Wachtersteig.

**Possible Summit Ascent:** From the top station on a path through the rock strewn east flank, finally beside the east ridge to the summit of the Grubigstein, 2233 m. (only for the surefooted).

# 25 Höllkopf, 2194 m

A summit "behind" the Marienbergjoch

**Biberwier – Marienbergjoch – Arzbödele – Höllkopf**

*Wamperter Schrofen in the Mieminger range.*

**Approach:** Biberwier, 989 m., holiday village in a picturesque situation among the knolls of the Fernpass prehistoric land slip.
**Start:** Bottom lift station at the southern end of Biberwier village.
**Parking:** At the bottom station or on the main road to the Fernpass.

**Walking Times:** Top station – Höllkopf good 2 hrs. On to Handschuhspitze, a little longer.
**Highest Point:** Höllkopf, 2194 m., poss. Handschuhspitze, 2319 m.
**Refreshments:** Marienbergjoch mountain restaurant.
**Of Interest:** Massive rock faces of Wamperter Schrofen.

Biberwier's unique and charming character is enhanced by the small knoll in the middle of the village – the result of a prehistoric land slip on the Fernpass. From the southern end of the village a series of lifts climbs up on to the Marienbergjoch. With their help, the wide saddle, with its breath-taking views south, can be reached without effort.

The onward path to the Höllkopf is soon in virtually unspoiled countryside. The summit is like a Belvedere which has been erected on the forward edge in the south of the Mieminger mountains. Another, almost unknown mountain, the Östliche Handschuhspitze, 2319 m., can be reached through the saddle, too. Its ascent, by means of a narrow footpath, requires a degree of surefootedness.

**To the Höllkopf:** Use both lifts to the top station, 1650 m., on the open ridge of the Bremstattkopf. From there into the nearby Marienbergjoch, 1789 m. On the other side briefly down then left across grass and dwarf pine covered slopes and past some picturesque outcrops and boulders to the Hölltörl, 2126 m. Then right at first across slate scree, over a steep ledge and left on to the broad summit.

**Handschuhspitze:** From the lift on to the western edge of the Marienbergjoch and then south below the ridge crossing some steep grass slopes to the summit (only a very narrow path).

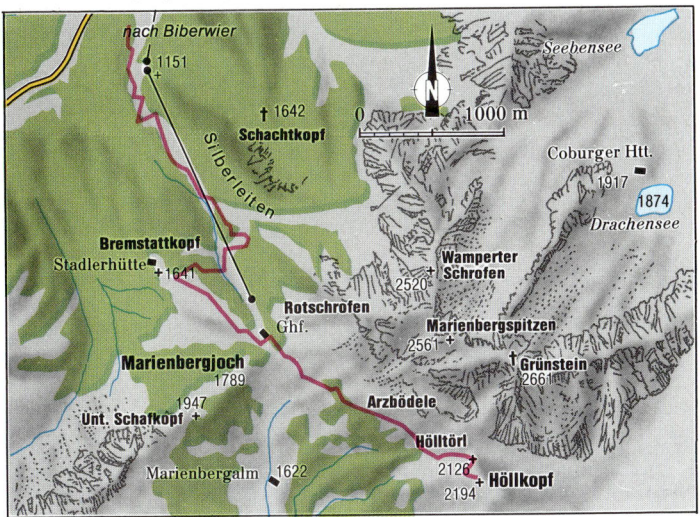

# 26 Coburger Hut and the Drachensee

Two contrasting possibilities

**Ehrwalder Alm – Seebenwald – Seebensee – Coburger Hut (Drachensee) – possible Return via Tajatörl and Brendlkar**

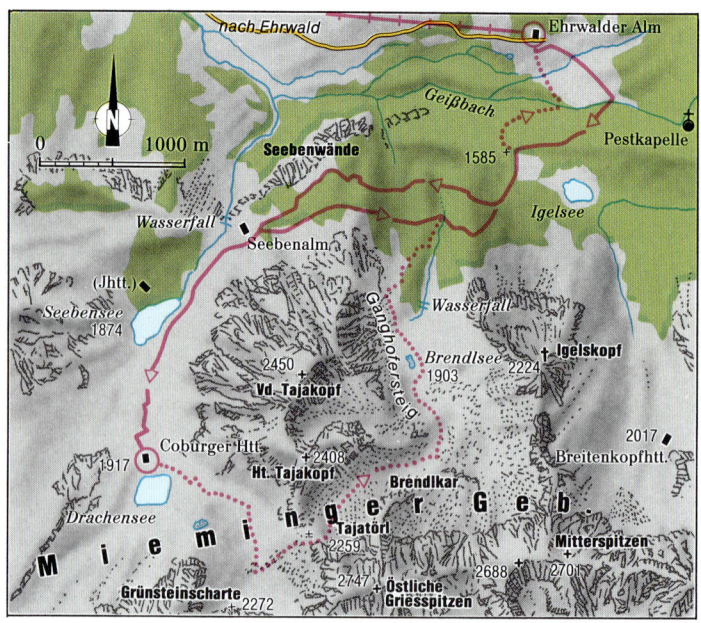

**Approach:** Ehrwald, 994 m., holiday village at the foot of the Zugspitze, magnificent, high alpine landscape.
**Start:** Ehrwalder Alm, 1500 m., top station of a small cabin lift. Bottom station at the upper, eastern edge of Ehrwald.
**Parking:** Large car park at the bottom station.
**Walking Times:** Ehrwalder Alm – Seebensee 1¾ hr., Seebensee – Coburger Hut ¾ hr. Poss. excursion to Hinteres Tajatörl 1 hr. Return from there 1½ hrs.
**Difficulty:** Good forest road to the Seebensee, then good but rocky tracks. Descent through Brendlkar on a narrow path.
**Highest Points:** Coburger Hut, 1917 m., poss. Hinteres Tajatörl, 2408 m.
**Refreshments:** Seebenalm, Coburger Hut, restaurants and cafés on Ehrwalder Alm.
**Of Interest:** Two picturesque mountain lakes and a view of the 800 m. high Wetterwand face.

*Thunder clouds above the Mieminger mountains (Tajakopf).*

Everyone should visit the Coburger Hut at least once. A friendly mountain lake and another harsh and uninviting, wonderful forests, alpine vegetation and a region of high, impressive mountains. Those are this route's enticing characteristics. A leisurely stroll to the Seebensee followed by a short climb up to the Coburger Hut.

**To the Coburger Hut:** From the Ehrwalder Alm into the valley and then right to a wooded shoulder on the opposite bank. A junction follows, either on the road, or above it on a small path to the Seebenalm. On to the nearby Seebensee and left along its E bank. Then over a ledge, covered in dwarf pine to the Coburger Hut, overlooking the Drachensee.

**Possible Return via the Tajatörl:** From the hut down to the Drachensee. Across the open ground and scree into Hinteres Tajatörl. Down through a small, scree cirque, left around the corner and out to the Brendlsee. Then over an overgrown step and down to the original ascent route in the Seebenwald.

# 27 Platt and Gatterl

The ultimate adventurous descent

**Schneefernerhaus (Zugspitze) – Platt – Gatterl – Feldernjöchl – Ehrwalder Alm – Ehrwald**

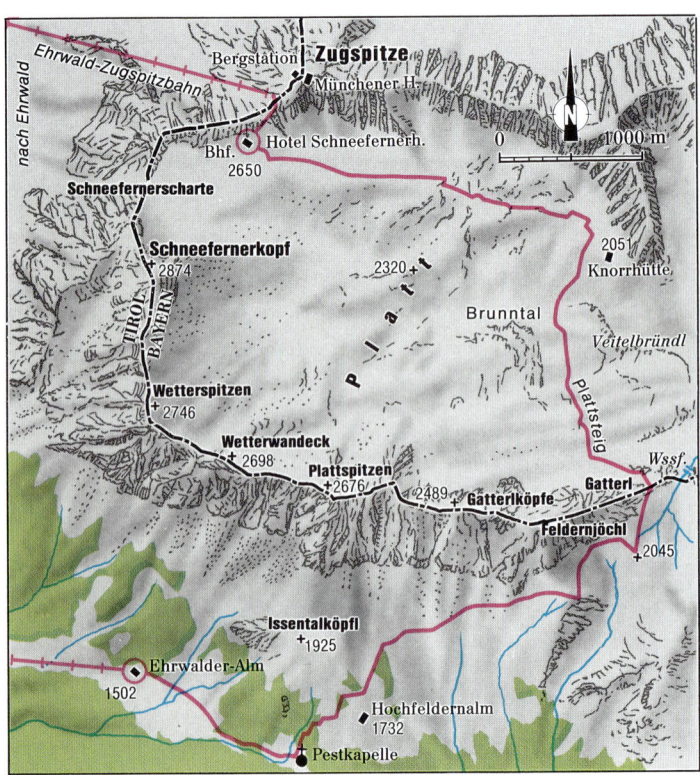

**Approach:** Ehrwald, 994 m., holiday village at the foot of the Zugspitze, magnificent, high alpine landscape.
**Start:** Schneefernerhaus, 2650 m., reached as follows: bus from Ehrwald to the bottom station of the Tiroler Zugspitzbahn and by this up to the hotel. Then either by lift to the Zugspitz summit or through the tunnel.
**Parking:** Where you can at Ehrwald.
**Walking Times:** Schneefernerhaus – Knorrhütte – Gatterl 2½ hrs. Gatterl – Ehrwal-

der Alm 1½ hrs.
**Difficulty:** Rough mountain paths, at Gatterl a short rock section (wire rope). Not to be attempted in fog!
**Highest Points:** Schneefernerhaus, 2650 m., Am Brand, 2130 m.
**Refreshments:** Knorr Hut, Hochfeldernalm, Ehrwalder Alm.
**Of Interest:** Zugspitze, vast limestone plateau, north face of Hochmanner.

*The Zugspitze massif from the south and Schneefernerkopf.*

The long descent from the Zugspitzplatt, through the Gatterl to Ehrwald leaves a variety of impressions. At first, the interminably long journey across the limestone plateau; then, the view from the Knorr Hut down into the deep Reintal, out of which rises the magnificent 1400 m. high north face of the Hochwanner. Yet an entirely different panorama is waiting at Gatterl, where the Mieminger range dominates, with its high dark walls in the east and, in the west a myriad of pinnacles and needles. Finally, descending over the velvety meadows to Ehrwald, one is amazed at the richness of the flowers and plants. (The lift down can be used!)

**From the Schneefernerhaus to Gatterl:** On the extreme north side of the Platt down to the Knorr Hut. Then a traverse along the Plattsteig followed by a short, sharp climb (wire rope) to the Gatterl.

**Onwards to the Ehrwalder Alm:** Briefly down and then up again to the similarly high Feldernjöchl, 2045 m. Traverse the slopes climbing slightly to a shoulder "Am Brand". Now a descending traverse across steep ground below Gatterlköpfe to the meadows of the Feldernalm. Finally west through a steep stream bed to the Ehrwalder Alm and either down across the meadows – or with the lift! – to Ehrwald.

## 28 Eibsee, 978 m.

A prehistoric landscape beneath the Zugspitze

**Around Germany's highest bathing lake**

**Approach:** Grainau, 758 m., village at the foot of the Waxensteinkamm. Station on the Bavarian Zugspitzbahn.
**Start:** East bank of the Eibsee, 980. m, reached on a wide road from Grainau, 4 km.
**Parking:** Large car park just before the east bank - fee paying!
**Walking Time:** Altogether 1½ hrs.

**Difficulty:** Ideally prepared footpath, almost entirely level.
**Highest Point:** Above the southern shore, 1020 m.
**Refreshments:** Only in the area of the car park.
**Of Interest:** North aspect of the Zugspitze and the rock faces of the Waxensteinkamm. Prehistoric rock slip.

*Left: Eibsee with the Zugspitze.*

This leisurely walk is a genuine sight-seeing tour. Not only is there the Zugspitze and its more than 1000 m. high rock faces and the six summits of the Waxensteinkamm; of unusual beauty is the northern shore of the Eibsee with its coves, nooks and crannies and the seven islands. In the forest one stumbles across fascinating little pools among an unbelievable jumble of knolls, hollows, gullies and boulders of every shape and size. This unique landscape and the Eibsee itself, are the result of a massive, prehistoric rock slide that broke off from the Zugspitze and Waxenstein massifs and which now covers an area of some ten square kilometres.

**Around the Eibsee:** The route offers the more attractive views if the south shore is chosen for the outward journey and the north shore for the way back.
From the hotel left and on a road along the shore to the outdoor swimming pool. On a wide track around a cove and slightly up now continuing on a footpath. Here, in the SW corner the sided fall steeply down to the water's edge. The ground flattens towards the western shore and after a relatively level section of shoreline, the area of the rock fall is reached. In this sharply undulating ground the track often diverts north into the forest to avoid the promontories and small peninsulas. A small bay, known as Untersee is crossed by a long bridge. Soon afterwards the hotel and car park are reached.

## 29 In the Höllental

A magnificent gorge at the foot of the Zugspitze

**Kreuzeck – Hupfleitenjoch – Knappenhäuser – Höllentalanger Hut – Höllentalklamm – Hammersbach**

**Approach:** Garmisch-Partenkirchen, 708 m., renowned holiday and winter sports resort in the wide basin of the Loisach with beautiful alpine scenery.
**Start:** Kreuzeck, 1621 m. Top station of the Kreuzeck lift. Reached from Garmisch on the road to Fernpass and Grainau. To the edge of village than left.
**Parking:** At the bottom station.
**Walking Times:** Kreuzeck – Hupfleitenjoch – Höllentalanger 2 hrs, Höllentalanger – Hammersbach 1½ hrs., Hammersbach – bottom station ½ hr.
**Difficulty:** Well prepared paths in sometimes steep and rocky ground.
**Highest Point:** Hupfleitenjoch, 1760 m.
**Refreshments:** Several places around Kreuzeck and Osterfelderkopf, Knappenhäuser, Höllentalanger Hut, cafés and restaurants in Hammersbach.
**Of Interest:** Magnificent mountain landscape, Höllentalklamm (narrow gorge).

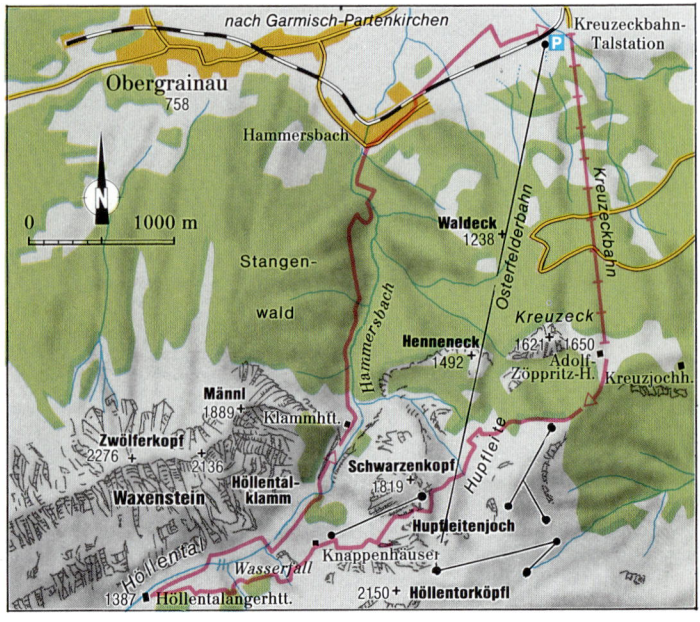

*On the way from Hupfleitenjoch into the Höllental.*

Today's route, although it crosses no peaks, should bring experiences which will be long remembered. On the path over the Hupfleitenjoch one cannot fail to be awed, above all, by the towering 1000 m. high flanks of the Waxenstein crest. On reaching Höllentalanger there is the stark contrast between the flat, green valley bottom and the grey massif of the Zugspitze high above. Then, finally, the path leads through the Höllentalklamm, which, with its plunging water masses and heaped, solid avalanche snow, is the most impressive of all the gorges.

**From Kreuzeck over the Hupfleitenjoch into the Höllental:** From Kreuzeck south down into a small, flat saddle. Junction. Then on the track right and west levelly along a rib across the slopes beneath the Osterfelderbahn. Upwards into the Hupfleitenjoch. On the other side, down steeply to the wonderfully situated Knappenhäuser. Finally, traversing easily down across the slope to Höllentalanger and the Alpine Club hut.

**Through the Höllentalklamm to Hammersbach:** Crossing the stream three times down the steeply, washed-out valley to the entrance of the Höllentalklamm. A steep descent through the gorge (several tunnels – wet – pay at the bottom) and down the gentler, lower valley to Hammersbach. On a path through meadows back to the bottom station.

# 30 Across the Bernadeinscharte into the Reintal

North face of the Alpspitze and Partnachklamm

**Osterfelderkopf – Bernadeinscharte – Stuibensee – Stuibenwald – Reintal – Partnachklamm – Garmisch-Partenkirchen station**

**Approach:** Garmisch-Partenkirchen, 708 m., renowned holiday and winter sports resort in the wide basin of the Loisach with beautiful alpine scenery.
**Start:** Osterfelderkopf, 2020 m., top station of the large cable car lift. Best way to the bottom station – with the Zugspitzbahn from Garmisch-Partenkirchen station.
**Parking:** Near the station.
**Walking Times:** Osterfelderkopf – Stuibensee 1 hr., Stuibensee – Reintal 1¾ hrs., Reintal – Garmisch-Partenkirchen station 1½ hrs.
**Difficulty:** The traverse of the north face demands surefootedness and a good sense of balance. If one avoids this section to the north the route, although rocky consists of good mountain paths.
**Highest Point:** Bernadeinscharte, 2110 m., Stuibensee, 1950 m.
**Refreshments:** Hochalm, restaurants near the Partnachklamm.
**Of Interest:** North face of the Alpspitze, Stuibensee, Partnachklamm.

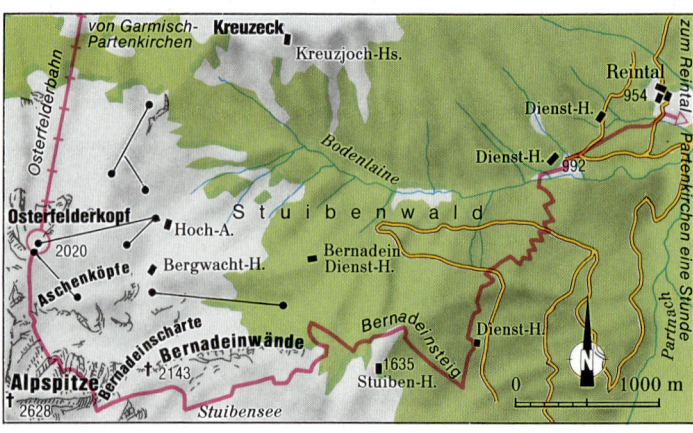

The footpaths and tracks criss-cross the countryside around the Kreuzeck like a spider's web. An abundance of possibilities is the result. We've chosen the most interesting route, although it is relatively long and challenging. There are alternatives for those who do not wish to walk so far, or prefer easier paths. People can put together their own day's itinerary. We'll make use of the Osterfelderbahn which, within a few minutes, brings us up to 2000 m. and into an imposing mountain landscape. Those not prone to vertigo can undertake the traverse of the "North Face Promenade", whilst the more circumspect leaves the Bernadeinwände to the north.

**From the Osterfelderkopf to Stuibenwand:** From the top station on almost level ground across to the rocks of the north wall of the Alpspitze. On an extremely well secured Via Ferrata traverse across to the Bernadeinscharte. Here to the left and on a grassy footpath down to the Stuibensee. Then NE across open ground and through dwarf pine descending to the Stuibenwald, where a path crosses. (This point can be reached as well by walking from the top station in the direction of Hochalm and then descending through the depression to the north of the Bernadeinwände). Take the transverse route right and up on to the Stuibenwand. (It is possible to turn left on this track, reaching the Kreuzeck in about 1 hr.)

**Return through the Reintal:** From the Stuibenwand about 10 min. in the direction of the Bock Hut, then left and on to a footpath descending for long period through the forest. Finally over the gully bed on the track into the Reintal. A level walk out of the valley then through the impressive Partnachklamm (gorge, fee!). The path through the valley to Partenkirchen seems to never end!

*At the Bernadeinscharte.*

# 31 Partnachklamm – Eckbauer – Wamberg

Interesting walk with variations

**Olympic Ski Stadium – Partnachklamm – Graseck – possible extension via Eckbauer to Wamberg**

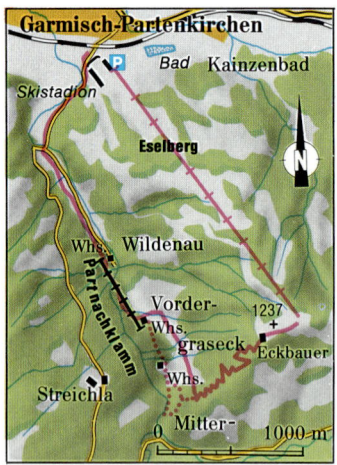

**Approach:** Garmisch-Partenkirchen, 708 m., renowned holiday and winter sports resort in the wide basin of the Loisach with beautiful alpine scenery.
**Start:** SE edge of the village at the Olympic Ski Stadium.
**Parking:** Large car parks on both sides of the stadium.
**Walking Times:** Car park – Graseck 1 hr., Graseck – Eckbauer 1 hr.; return via Wamberg 1¼ hrs.
**Difficulty:** Good footpaths.
**Highest Point:** Vordergraseck, 890 m., poss. Eck (Eckbauer), 1237 m.
**Refreshments:** Restaurants at the entrance to the Partnachklamm, at Vordergraseck, Eck and in Wamberg.
**Of Interest:** Partnachklamm, impressive rock gorge with absolutely vertical walls, about 1 km. long.

Anyone already visiting Werdenfelser Land should in no way fail to include the two magnificent rock gorges, the Höllentalklamm (see Tour 29) and the Partnachklamm, in their programme. In the Partnachklamm, the water flows relatively peacefully through the deep bed of the gorge.

**The Shortest Lap:** From the stadium along the road beside the river Partnach and through the gorge (fee). At the far end a large rock fail in 1991 blocked the Partnach forming a small lake. The path avoids this section by means of a tunnel. At the end of the gorge left and upwards on a good footpath to Vordergraseck with superb views across to the rocky summits of the Wetterstein. Back to the valley by lift.

**The Medium Lap:** As above to Vordergraseck. Climb further on good paths to the open shoulder at Eck (Eckbauer) with its far better allround views. Back to the valley in the cable car.

**The Longest Lap:** As for the first lap, through the narrow gorge. Now, however, on the right side of the brook up to the restaurant Partnachalm and

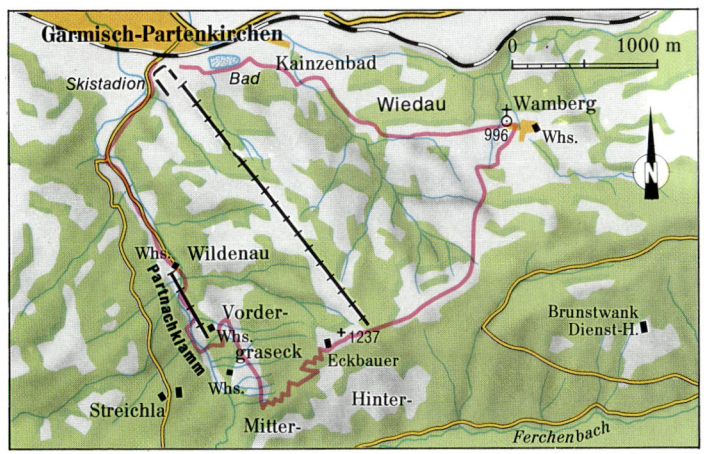

then slightly down towards Hoher Steg (bridge over the gorge). On the other side up to Vordergraseck and on to Eck. E on the ridge, then NE descending to the small mountain village of Wamberg, 996 m. Back along a small road to the stadium.

*The north face of the Wetterstein with the Wamberg ridge in the foreground.*

# 32 Kranzberg, Grünkopf and Ederkanzel

A mountain walk around the violin manufacturing village of Mittenwald

**Hoher Kranzberg – Ferchensee – Grünkopf – Ederkanzel – Lautersee – Mittenwald**

*The Untere Wettersteinspitze.*

**Approach:** Mittenwald, 913 m, pretty market village and lively holiday resort in the Isar valley, lovely baroque church, renowned for its violin workshops.
**Start:** Hoher Kranzberg, 1391 m., top station of the lift. Bottom station at NW end of Mittenwald
**Parking:** Car park at the bottom station of the Kranzbergbahn.
**Walking Times:** Hoher Kranzberg – Ferchensee – Grünkopf 2¼ hrs., Grünkopf – Ederkanzel – Lautersee 1¼ hrs., Lautersee – Mittenwald ½ hr.
**Difficulty:** Good mountain paths, only on the east side of the Grünkopf is the way steeper and alpine-like (detour poss.).
**Highest Points:** Hoher Kranzberg, 1391 m.; Grünkopf, 1588 m.
**Refreshments:** Restaurants at Ferchensee, on Ederkanzel and at Lautersee.
**Of Interest:** Two mountain and forest lakes. Forestry Teaching Trail.

This round-trip encompasses all those interesting places to the west of Mittenwald which deserve a visit. Among them is the Hoher Kranzberg, which stands out like a Belvedere with fine, uninterrupted views of the Karwendel as well as the Wetterstein. Included, too, are two large lakes, nestling in meadows and guarded by forests – and untouched by the ubiquitous motor car. A more alpine tone is set by the Grünkopf although, from below, it is hardly impressive. Nevertheless, between 1400 m. and 1500 m. high, a steep step waits in ambush, demanding a certain amount of mountaineering skill. The Ederkanzel, too, must be mentioned, with its unique views down into four valleys.

**From Kranzberg on to the Grünkopf:** From Kranzberg across the broad summit (direction of Untere Wettersteinspitze) to an edge then descending through forest to the Ferchensee. Right or left around the lake to its southern shore. Here a track branches off west (Obere Wettersteinspitze), which after about half-an-hour forks again in several directions. Take the upper-most branch to the left and, mainly through woods, on a small path to the summit.

**Return to Mittenwald:** Across the east ridge with a steep step down, then through extensive, flat forest to the Ederkanzel (also possible from Ferchensee). Now down to Mittenwald or, more rewarding, to the Lautersee and along its beautiful eastern shore. Then, either through pine forest past the Felseneck, or through the Laintalschlucht.

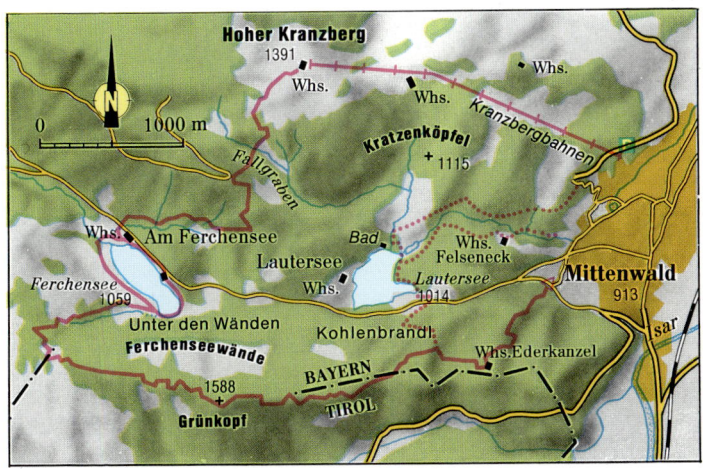

# 33 Around the Schartenkopf

On the northern Arnspitze massif

**Klammbrücke – Gletscherschliff – poss. Leutaschklamm – Riedbergscharte – Restaurant "Mühle" – Klammbrücke (or Riedbergscharte – Große Arnspitze)**

**Approach:** Mittenwald, 913 m, attractive market town and lively holiday resort in the Isar valley, lovely baroque church, renowned for its violin building.
**Start:** Gorgebridge, 1010 m., bridge over the Leutascher Ache, where the meadows of Unterleutasch begin. North of the Customs Post.
**Parking:** South of the bridge.
**Walking Times:** Gorgebridge – Gletscherschliff-Restaurant – Riedbergscharte 2¼ hrs., detour to Leutaschklamm ¾ hr.; return 1 hr. poss. Große Arnspitze from Restaurant "Mühle" 3¼ hrs.
**Difficulty:** Mountain tracks without any problem areas. (Tour of the Arnspitze – steep summit with protected sections.)
**Highest Points:** Riedbergscharte, 1454 m., poss. Große Arnspitze, 2196 m.
**Refreshments:** Gletscherschliff-Restaurant, Restaurant "Mühle".
**Of Interest:** Leutaschklamm.

Before the northern flank of the Arnspitze massif drop steeply into the Leutaschklamm, it offers one last rounded, forest-covered summit. This is the Schartenkopf, 1616 m., around which we will be walking today. The paths are shady and although there are steeper sections, it is generally a rather leisurely tour. However, who has heard of this rewarding circuit at all? Don't forget your passport – the walk crosses the Austrian border.

The more experienced mountaineer will be attracted by the Große Arnspitze, a beautiful, solitary pyramid. The most interesting route is that described below – from the north across the open Achterköpfe. However, the summit demands surefootedness and there are sections which are secured by wire rope.

*The Arnspitze massif from the north.*

**Around the Schartenkopf:** South of the bridge on the forestry road and east parallel to the gorge. Then on a smaller path across the wooded slopes to the Gletscherschliff-Restaurant. Detour (steeply down the forestry road) to the Leutaschklamm (fee!). Just below the restaurant the footpath branches off to the Riedbergscharte (signed) which is reached ascending diagonally through the forest. On the other side steeply down to the Restaurant "Mühle", then on the road back to the car park – 1 km.

**Ascent of the Große Arnspitze:** From Restaurant "Mühle" steeply up into the Riedbergscharte. Then south along or beside the Achterköpfe ridge to a height of about 1900 m. Left across the steep grassy slopes, through a gully and up to the Arnspitzhütterl (shelter). Now west over steep slopes and several rugged sections to the summit cross.

# 34 The Puittal

A valley with three interesting possibilities

## Gasse – Puitbach – Puiteck – Scharnitzjoch – poss. Gehrenspitze or Söller Pass

**Approach:** Lehner, a small village NE of Oberleutasch, 1115 m., a sunny holiday resort.
**Start:** At the northern end of Lehner.
**Parking:** At the side of the road.
**Walking Times:** Lehner – Puitalm 1½ hrs.; Puitalm – Söller Pass 1¾ hrs.; Scharnitzjoch – Gehrenspitze 1¼ hrs.
**Difficulty:** Puittal and Scharnitzjoch – good mountain paths; to the Söller Pass high rock step, surefootedness required. Gehrenspitze, narrow path, in parts on very steep, grassy slopes.
**Highest Points:** Scharnitzjoch, 2048 m., Söller Pass, 2211 m, Gehrenspitze, 2367 m.
**Refreshments:** None in the vicinity of the Puittal.
**Of Interest:** Impressive rocky landscape above a green valley floor. Views on to the S faces of the Schüsselkarspitze.

The two utterly contrasting valleys of the Puittal and Bergltal, are separated by the Öfelekopf, 2479 m., a towering, solitary massif. The Bergltal impresses by its harshness, the other with its soft, park-like meadowland which reaches high up its valley floor. Just the walk to the Puitalm is rewarding in itself. The more adventurous, however, can choose from other possibilities – a leisurely crossing of the Scharnitzjoch, or an ascent of the Gehrenspitze.

**To the Puitalm:** From Lehner on the forestry road to Puitbach. Across the bridge, then left on a good, but sometimes rocky, footpath through open forest to the broad Puitalm.

*The Leutascher Dreitorspitze above the Puittal.*

**Into the Scharnitzjoch:** On the main track, across the valley floor and up the strongly grooved slopes, without difficulty, into the Joch. From there, a track offers a descent across the Wangalm to Klamm/Oberleutasch (1¾ hrs., rocky paths).

**Ascent of the Gehrenspitze:** From the Scharnitzjoch, a mountain path leads up on to the peak, 2367 m., with its steep, impressive north wall plunging directly from the summit, into the Puittal 500 m. below. Pass the Erinnerungshütte (hut, no refreshments!) and over a shoulder on to the massif. Then on a narrow path up very steep, south facing slopes to the summit.

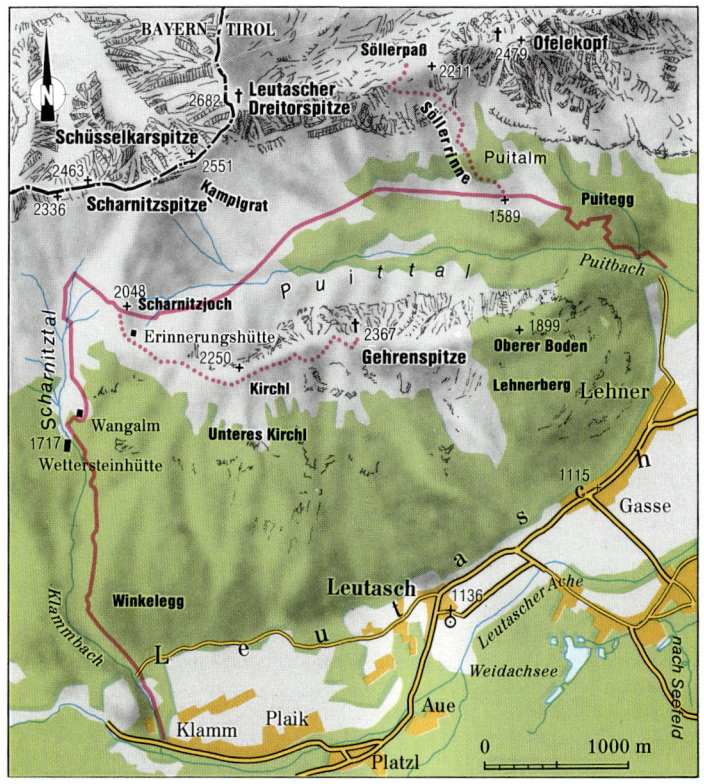

# 35 Schönberg or Predigtstuhl

Belvederes on the southern side of the Wetterstein

**Gaistal – Hemermooswiesen – Loatental – Rotmoosalm – Schönberg**

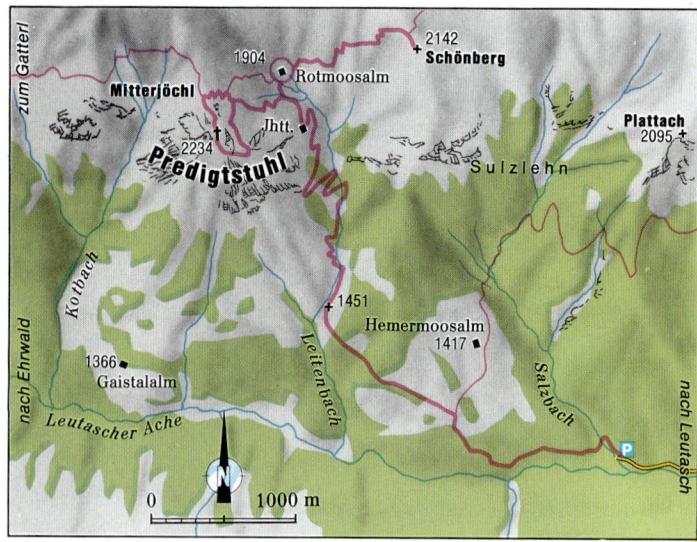

**Approach:** Oberleutasch, 1172 m., quiet, sunny holiday village in the long, meadowed valley of the river Leutasch.
**Start:** Bridge over the Salzbach in the Gaistal, 1220 m., some 2 km. from Leutasch/gorge along the valley.
**Parking:** Before the bridge.
**Walking Times:** The bridge – Rotmoosalm 2¼ hrs.; to the summit about 1 hr.
**Difficulty:** To Schönberg, narrow paths in the upper reaches, but without difficulty. To Predigtstuhl, very rocky ground but not exposed.
**Highest Points:** Schönberg, 2142 m., or Predigtstuhl, 2223 m.
**Refreshments:** Possibly Hemermoosalm.

The Hochwanner, 2744 m., is the main peak along the south ridge of the Wetterstein mountains. Its southern flank plunges almost 1000 m. down into the Gaistal. The Predigtstuhl, a relatively prominent summit protrudes from these steep slopes. It is the finest observation point in the whole valley. However, the route to the Predigtstuhl is a rare example of badly though-out track preparation. Although there is a path across the steep, grassy east

*The Hemermoosalm, with Schönberg left in the middle distance. In the background, the Reintalschrofen and the Teufelsgrat ridge.*

flank, a far more attractive, but not more difficult route would have been the climb over the ribs and grooves of the north ridge. However, those who prefer a more comfortable summit assault will content themselves with the unimpressive, grassy Schönberg.

**To the Rotmoosalm:** From the bridge along the valley road for about 10 mins., to where the road to Hemermoosalm (Hämmersmoosalm) branches off. On this road to the meadows. At a signpost left on an old forest track into the Loatental. Across the stream and climbing for a reasonable distance until joining a road which has been driven through the countryside with no regard for it whatsoever. On this road to the Rotmoosalm.

**Schönberg:** A grassy knoll above the pasture. On the path into a saddle between the knoll and the main feature. Then along the ridge to the summit.

**Predigtstuhl:** It appears as a mixture of grass and rock west of the Rotmoosalm. Follow the markers across the meadowed slopes into a saddle north of the Predigtstuhl. Either before the saddle left, following the markers through a steep and awkward gully, or from the saddle itself, up and along the ribbed northern ridge.

# 36 Niedere Munde, 2059 m.

A saddle with surprising views to the south

### Gaistal – Meadows of the Gaistalalm – Niedere Munde

**Approach:** Oberleutasch, 1172 m., quiet, sunny holiday village in the long, meadowed valley of the river Leutasch.
**Start:** Bridge over the Salzbach in the Gaistal, 1220 m., some 2 km. from Leutasch/gorge along the valley.
**Parking:** Before the bridge.

**Walking Times:** Into the valley 1¼ hrs., climb to the saddle 2¼ hrs.
**Difficulty:** In the upper section, narrow, rocky, but good tracks.
**Highest Point:** Niedere Munde, 2059 m.
**Refreshments:** Gaistalalm.

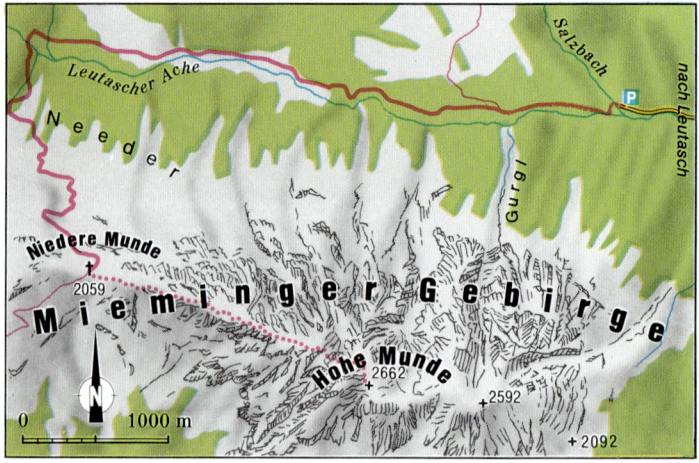

There are only two distinctive, wider saddles in the 20 km. long main ridge of the Mieminger mountains. One is the Marienbergjoch (Tour 24) and the other, the Niedere Munde, otherwise known as Niedermundesattel. The latter, today's objective is protected by two particularly impressive mountain features. Hochwand, 2721 m., and Hohe Munde, 2662 m. The ascent falls into two markedly different sections. Up to the Gaistalalm one walks on a wide forestry track, and then, all of a sudden, a small, but good, mountain track leads steeply up to the saddle. Surprising, wide panorama of the Stubai Alps. Special to this walk is that, despite much of it being in a valley and forest, the views of the mountains are virtually uninterrupted.

**The Ascent:** From the bridge over the Salzbach along the road into the valley. It remains above the stream and leads through woods and across meadows. Beyond the meadows of the Gaistalalm a further 400 m. through the woods to a small stream flowing from the right. A road junction follows straight away. Left and down over the Gaistalbach. Across the bridge the track to the Niedere Munde branches off. Through the forest (watch the markers) and over the meadows, between dwarf pine and directly up to the saddle. An uninterrupted view can be obtained by climbing up along the initially wide ridge to the east. After a pine-covered false summit the grassy ridge is reached.

**Hohe Munde:** Can be reached from here on a typically alpine track in about 2 hrs. It is only for experienced mountaineers who are at home on steep, friable rocky ground (easy rock climbing, wire ropes).

*Hohe Munde from the Feldernalm.*

# 37 Reither Spitze, 2374 m.

Different possibilities on Seefeld's highest mountain

**Either: Reith – Schartlehner-Restaurant – Nördlinger Hut – Reither Spitze; or a round trip from the Härmelekopf**

**Approach:** Either Reith, 1130 m, village in a lovely position high above the Inn valley. Or Seefeld, 1180 m, well-known, rather worldly holiday and winter sports resort (Olympic Games), situated in a broad, sunny basin.

**Start:** Either the church square in Reith, or the top station of the Härmelekopf, 2224 m., reached from NE edge of Seefeld via the funicular and cable car.

**Parking:** Limited parking in Reith. Large car park at the bottom station in Seefeld.

**Walking Times:** Reith – Nördlinger Hut 3¼ hrs., Hut – Reither Spitze 25 min.; round tour of Härmelekopf 2 hrs.

**Difficulty:** Ascent from Reith to the Hut on good tracks. The upper sections are steep and rugged and require surefootedness and experience.

**Highest Point:** Reither Spitze, 2374 m., or Seefelder Spitze 2221 m.

**Refreshments:** Nördlinger Hut, Roß Hut.

**Of Interest:** Wild and fascinating rock formations, towers and pinnacles. Magnificent long-range views.

How much are you prepared to pay to avoid a climb of 800 (vertical) meters? The ride up the mountain with the lifts from Seefeld to the Härmelekopf is – for a vertical difference of only 800 m – particularly expensive. It depends on you – ride up with the lift and be faced by a relatively short summit tour. Or, start down in Reith and enjoy the walk up with its ever widening and improving views – especially towards the Inn valley. The Reither Spitze itself, is worth a visit in any case, as it is one of the finest vantage points in the area covered by the guide.

*The Nördlinger Hut on the way to the Reither Spitze.*

Equally, the Nördlinger Hut, situated at the southern foot of the rocky summit, is not only the highest Alpine Club hut in the Karwendel, but one of the most attractively positioned.

**Ascent from Reith:** From the church straight up to the edge of the forest. Then left for a reasonable distance through wonderful larch and birch trees. Up through open forest for some way, then left and slightly down to the – occasionally open – Schartlehner-Restaurant. Over a dwarf pine covered slope then below the grassy ridge to the Nördlinger Hut. Then left of the edge up steep, rugged, but not dangerous ground (a little rock climbing) to the summit cross on the Reither Spitze.

**The Summit Circuit:** From the Härmelekopf traverse across the very steep slopes to the Nördlinger Hut. Climb the Reither Spitze as above. Then north-west, steep with protection and a ladder down into the saddle in front of the Härmelekopf and right down into the Reither Kar. Now, either straight up the other side to the Seefelder Spitze, 2221 m., and the ridge walk to the Seefelder Joch (very steep, grassy going in parts), or a traverse across equally steep slopes along the Schönangersteig to the Seefelder Joch or the Roß Hut (top station).

# 38 Eppzirltal

In the midst of the wild pinnacles and towers of the Erlspitz group

**Gießenbach – Gießenbachtal – Eppzirltal – Eppzirler Alm**

**Approach:** Gießenbach, 1012 m., a newly developed community between Scharnitz and Seefeld at the mouth of the stream of the same name.
**Start:** Mouth of the Gießenbachtal, 1012 m.
**Parking:** Small car park behind the railway crossing.
**Walking Times:** Gießenbach – Eppzirler Alm 2 hrs., poss. excursion to Eppzirlscharte 1¾ hrs.
**Difficulty:** Easy walking to the Alm on a farm road; to Eppzirlscharte steep path on scree. The Freiungen-Höhenweg is a fixed rope route.
**Highest Points:** Eppzirler Alm, 1459 m., poss. Eppzirlscharte, 2102 m; poss. Freiungen, 2332 m.
**Refreshments:** Eppzirler Alm; poss. Solsteinhaus.
**Of Interest:** Gießenbach gorge, wild primeval rock landscape.

The Erlspitz group is the last, western appendage of the Karwendel mountains. This almost 10 km. long summit ridge is a jumble of pinnacles, needles and clefts (a result of the vertical strata) and surrounds the Eppzirltal like a horse-shoe. In the middle of this horse-shoe nestles the Eppzirler Alm. From Gießenbach one can reach this little café up the long valley. At first is a fascinating gorge, then through a narrow, wooded valley and finally crossing a broad, sometimes rocky ground, sometimes mountain pasture and always with the bizarre, rocky backdrop in view. Anyone, not satisfied with this, somewhat contemplative, walk can climb farther into the more alpine region, across the Eppzirlscharte or, for that matter, attempt the Via Ferrata of the Freiungen-Höhenweg.

**From Gießenbach to the Alm:** At the saw mill over the railway and on the forest/farm road up into the valley; walking at first through a charming gorge, then in a wooded valley and finally, over scree and grass to the café.

**Crossing the Eppzirlscharte (notch):** Over the meadows up the valley (watch the markers) and among dwarf pine into the Kuhloch, a broad scree-covered cirque at the head of the valley. Up a track above the scree slopes and through a small boulder-filled gully on to the notch. On the other side through the conglomeration of pinnacles and towers then steeply down to the Solsteinhaus; from there down to Hochzirl railway station.

**The Freiungen-Höhenweg (Via Ferrata):** This rocky path is one of the most interesting routes in the Karwendel. Surefootedness is vital; in parts it is protected. Undertaken best as a circuit: Nördlinger Hut (Tour 37) – Ursprungsattel – Freiungen – Eppzirlscharte – Eppzirltal.

*The Kuhlochspitze seen from the Eppzirltal.*

# 39 Mittagkopf and Zäunlkopf

A quiet walk with an imposing backdrop

**Gießenbach – Mittagkopf – Zäunlkopf – Oberbrunnalm – Karltal – Gießenbachtal – Gießenbach**

**Approach:** Gießenbach, 1012 m., a newly developed community between Scharnitz and Seefeld at the mouth of the stream of the same name.
**Start:** Mouth of the Gießenbachtal, 1012 m.
**Parking:** Small car park behind the railway crossing.
**Walking Times:** Gießenbach – Mittagkopf 1¾ hrs., Mittagkopf – Zäunlkopf – Oberbrunnalm ¾ hr.; descent 1 hr.
**Difficulty:** Small, sometimes indistinct paths with no difficulties or risks.
**Highest Points:** Mittagkopf, 1636 m, the shoulder on Zäunlkopf, 1746 m.
**Refreshments:** Oberbrunnalm.
**Of Interest:** Gießenbach gorge.

Today's walk is one of the most solitary and least known in the entire region. From the valley these summits do not catch the eye, for they are surrounded on three sides by the domineering rocky peaks of the Karwendel. The fourth side of the circle is filled by the tops of the Arnspitze. But it is just this situation which gives the tour its individual original magic. One is walking almost on his own private mountain, whilst at the same time, able to enjoy the grandeur of the surrounding giants. At one stage the Wetterstein can be seen, then the Brunnsteinspitze and later the Karwendel with the Pleisenspitze and Hochgleiresch. Finally, our gaze is trapped by the pinnacles and towers of the Erlspitz crests.

**Ascent:** A few minutes only along the road into the Gießenbachtal. At the first bridge left on to a footpath and left again up on to the ridge. Through the woods north of the Marendköpfl to the top station of the Scharnitz ski lifts. Continue the route east along the left, lower edge of the clearing. On a small path up through open forest, across glades and clearings to the Mittagkopf. Then a few meters down and through mainly dwarf pine, on to the south shoulder of the Zäunlkopf. South of this summit and remaining on the slope traverse across to the meadows around the Oberbrunnalm.

**Descent:** Back on the road through Karltal and Gießenbachtal.

*Left: On the way into Gießenbachtal.*

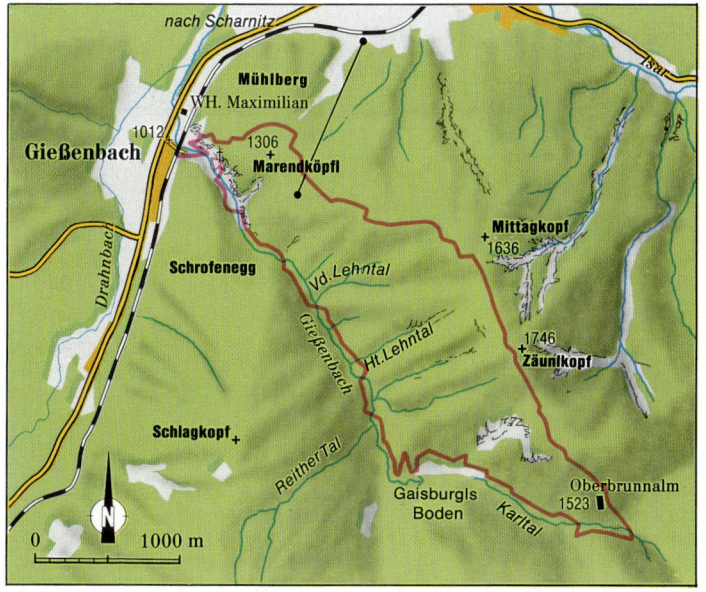

# 40 Pleisen Hut, 1757 m.

The Karwendel belvedere

**Scharnitz – Pürzlkapelle – Karwendelsteg – Wasserlegraben – Pleisen Hut**

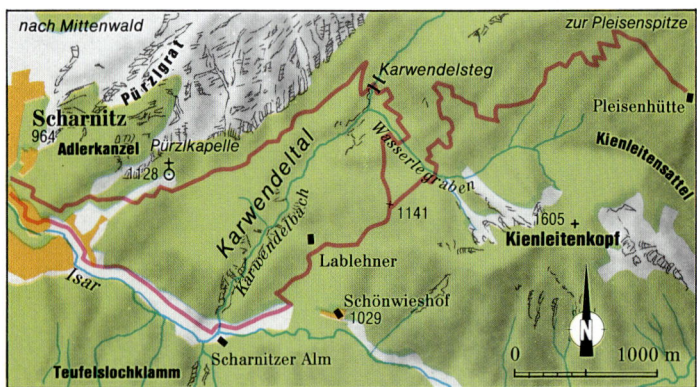

**Approach:** Scharnitz, 964 m., the first village in Tyrol, in the lovely valley of the young river Isar.
**Start:** From the church along Eisackweg and Hinterautalstraße to the Isar bridge SE of the village.
**Parking:** Car park over the bridge, 971 m.
**Walking Times:** Scharnitz – Karwendelsteg 1 hr., Karwendelsteg – Pleisen Hut 2 hrs.
**Difficulty:** Roads and good paths.
**Highest Points:** Pleisen Hut, 1757 m., poss. Pleisenspitze, 2547m.
**Refreshments:** Pleisen Hut.
**Of Interest:** Views on to the magnificent north faces of the Gleiersch group, the gorge at Karwendelsteg.

A short excursion into the sanctuary of the high Karwendel. The private hut perches in open ground on the south west ridge of the Pleisenspitze. Thus, one is blessed with uninterrupted views to the west, with the Wetterstein and the Mieminger mountains, and south to the entire Gleiersch group, the Solsteine and the Erlspitz range.

However, the particular spectacle are the north faces of the Hochgleiersch, Jägerkarspitze and Praxmarerkarspitze, towering 900 m. high on the opposite side of the Gleiersch valley. They consist of sombre, crumbling rock walls which, because of their extreme friability, are shunned by today's rock climbers. The eastern section of the Praxmarerkarspitze's north face is also known as the Melzerwand, after Otto Melzer, the Innsbruck climber, who was killed there in dramatic circumstances.

**The Ascent:** The route over the Karwendelsteg, described below, is longer, but far more interesting, than the direct route. From the car park north towards the houses at Inrain. At the second junction right and up to the Pürzlkapelle. Easily down to a small road and another 1 km. up the valley in open ground. Now down and right on to the Karwendelsteg and an impressive gorge. A short climb then on forestry roads over the ditch to a junction where the direct route is joined. Sharp left there through the forest to Berglehne and diagonally right across the dwarf pine covered slope to the hut.

**The Descent:** Back to the road junction. Now straight on past Lablehner and down into the Isar valley. Out of the valley on the road and back to the car park.

**Possible Summit Ascent:** Experienced mountaineers can reach the Pleisenspitze, 2547 m., in about 2 hrs. Narrow track and route markings. A detour into Vorderkar is recommended in any case, where there are large dolines (caves) to be seen.

*Pleisenspitze from the south-west.*

# 41 Hochland Hut, 1623 m.

Beneath the Tiefkarspitze and Wörner

**Mittenwald – Ochsenboden – Mittereck – Hochland Hut – poss. Steinkarlkopf; or Karwendelbahn – Dammkar – Hochland Hut**

**Approach:** Mittenwald, 912 m., pretty market village and lively holiday resort in the Isar valley, lovely baroque church, known for violin building.

**Start:** Either the bottom station, 930 m., or the top station, 2240 m., of the Karwendel cable car.

**Parking:** Large car park at the bottom station with direct access from the bypass, east of Mittenwald.

**Walking Times:** Mittenwald – Hochland Hut 2½ hrs.; top station – Dammkar – Hochland Hut 2½ hrs., Hochland Hut – Steinkarlkopf 1¼ hrs.

**Difficulty:** Between Mittenwald and Hochland Hut mountain paths with no dangerous sections. Descent into the Dammkar, smooth stones and scree. Surefootedness needed.

**Highest Points:** Hochland Hut, 1623 m.; Linderspitze, 2372 m.; poss. Steinkarlkopf, 1981 m.

**Refreshments:** Hochland Hut (not always), Dammkar Hut, Top Station.

**Of Interest:** Impressive mountain scenery. A cable car up especially steep ground.

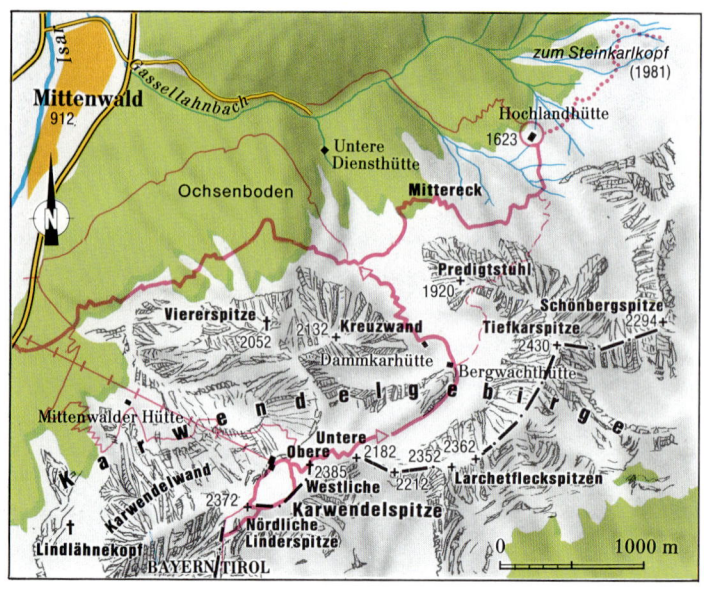

*Tiefkarspitze and the Larchetfleckspitzen.*

Here we again offer two completely different possibilities. You can either walk up from Mittenwald, over various forest paths, to the Hochland Hut – a mountain walk with no particular problems. Or, you can swing up in the large cable car, above breathtaking views, to the Karwendelgrube and pay a lightning visit to the Linderspitze, 2372 m., followed by a descent through the Dammkar to the Hochland Hut. On this walk you will discover a sombre but impressive corner of the mountains, filled with scree and overlooked by savage rock towers.

**Ascent from Mittenwald:** 300 m. north of the car park, under the bypass and on the other side left. Soon afterwards the path to the Hochland Hut branches off. On this path diagonally up through the woods and under the Dammkar. Then east on level ground to the Mittereck where the ground steepens. Cross the floor of the cirque to the already visible hut.

**Traverse from the Karwendelbahn:** From the top station one can reach the Linderspitze in 20 min. (2372 m., beautiful views south). Then, either over the Dammkarscharte (surefootedness required) or through the tunnel to the upper end of the Dammkar. At first on grass, then over a steeper section down into the lower cirque and to the Dammkar Hut. Below the hut, the path joins the direct route from Mittenwald.

**Detour to the Steinkarlkopf:** This belvedere sits on the ridge north of the Wörner. From the Hochland Hut east and level, then steeper up the slopes to the Steinkarl ridge and left to the summit, with its superb views.

# 42 Seinsköpfe, 1961 m.

A belvedere overlooking six lakes

## Krün – Hüttlebachklamm – Schwarzkopf – Felsenköpfl – Seinsköpfe

**Approach:** Krün, 875 m., a sprawling holiday resort on the upper Isar.
**Start:** Isar bridge at Krün.
**Parking:** Near the bridge.
**Walking Times:** Krün – Schwarzkopf 1 hr., Schwarzkopf – Seinsköpfe 2 hrs.
**Difficulty:** Good path.
**Highest Point:** Östlicher Seinskopf, 1961 m.
**Refreshments:** None.

*Seinsköpfe high above Krün.*

The Soiern range of the Karwendel mountains pushes a ridge towards the west which ends high above the Isar valley at Krün. This ridge contains the Seinsköpfe. From its high, exposed situation looking down on the picturebook landscape, with its wooded knolls, meadows, nestling lakes and handsome villages, is like looking out of an aircraft.

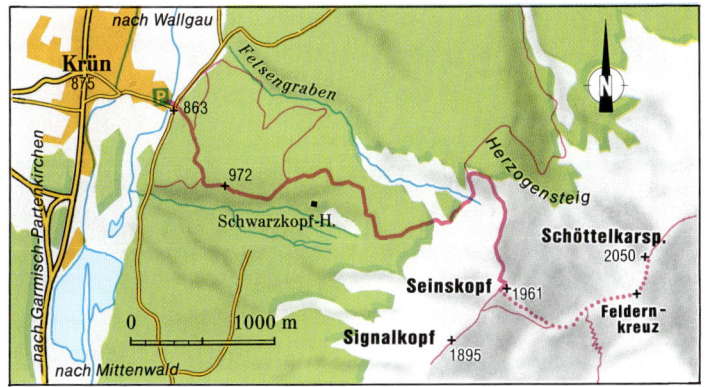

The Seinsköpfe rise 1100 m. above the valley although, in spite of this, the walk up requires only three hours. The path begins rather like a promenade, changing later to a narrow, good track which heads straight up to the summit. It leads through woods, across glades and over the Schwarzkopf, 1220 m., an observation point with views of Mittenwald and the Wetterstein. The mountain consists of several summits, the highest of which lies along the eastern ridge. However, the view we describe is to be enjoyed only from the westernmost peak.

**The Ascent:** Across the Isar bridge at Krün. Now, either immediately right and upwards through the woods, past the water tank to a weather shelter at the edge of the Hüttlegraben. Or, right along the forestry road and then upwards through the ditch (signed "Klamm") itself. Through open forest on to the Schwarzkopf (view point). On through the woods to about 1500 m., then left and across two rocky ditches on to a shoulder – track junction. Pass a small rocky knoll and keeping mainly to the right of the ridge up into an area of dwarf pine. Over a grassy slope on to the main ridge and either, left to the highest point, or right to the western summit.

**Possible Mountain Tour:** From the Seinsköpfe a small track leads to the Feldernkreuz, for much of the way traversing the very steep southern flank. From here through a small, sharply cut notch to reach the Schöttelkarspitze; a good hour's walk. Surefootedness is needed on the rough ground. Descent into the Soiernkessel see Tour 43.

## 43 Fischbachalm und Soiernkessel

In King Ludwig's hunting grounds

**Wallgau – Isarsteg – Fischbachalm – "Lakaiensteig" – Soiernhäuser – poss. Schöttelkarspitze**

**Approach:** Wallgau, 866 m., holiday resort on N rim of the wide Isar basin with fine views of the Karwendel and Wetterstein mountains.
**Start:** South-east edge of Wallgau (Isarstraße).
**Parking:** In the vicinity of the start.
**Walking Times:** Wallgau – Fischbachalm 2¼ hrs., Fischbachalm – Soiernhäuser 1 hr., poss. Soiernhäuser – Schöttelkarspitze 1¼ hrs.

**Difficulty:** An easy walk to Fischbachalm, "Lakaiensteig", narrow, on sometimes rocky ground. Schöttelkarspitze presents no further difficulties.
**Highest Points:** Fischbachalm, 1405 m.; Soiernhäuser, 1616 m.; Schöttelkarspitze, 2049 m.
**Refreshments:** Fischbachalm, Soiernhäuser.
**Of Interest:** Rocky mountain cirque with two lakes.

*The Schöttelkarspitze from the north.*

There have always been the privileged! In the old days the eminent and distinguished around the Bavarian King would ride up from Krün to the Fischbachalm; then through the Hundstall and into the picturesque cirque of the Soiernkessel with its lakes and fringe of brittle rock. The servants, of course, walked up. Their memory is honoured by the "Lakaienweg" (Footmen's Path), the shortest route from the Fischbachalm to the royal hunting lodges in the Soiernkessel and which traverses the gully-scarred slopes below the Schöttelköpfe, demanding a certain surefootedness. Today there is a road of the unbelievable breadth through the Fischbach saddle, over which again, only a few privileged can drive. In fact, everyone can walk to the Fischbachalm with little effort. However, the way on to the Soiernkessel remains the preserve of the more experienced and fitter. The more tenacious (poss. overnight stay in the Soiernhäuser) will naturally not allow an ascent of the Schöttelkarspitze to escape them.

**To the Fischbachalm:** Across the Isarsteg over gravelly ground to the left. On the left side of a stream and up through woods to the wide forestry road ascending from Krün (of course, one could start at Krün). On this road left through the woods for some considerable time, to the Fischbachalm.

**The "Lakaiensteig":** An interesting, well prepared and in the steeper parts protected footpath. Towards the end briefly up the Soiernhäuser situated some 70 m. above the lakes.

**Schöttelkarspitze:** Along the old bridle path with no real problems (unless the track has slipped!) towards the rocky summit and steeply up to the cross.

## 44 Krepelschrofen and Maxhütte

A half-circle around Wallgau

**Wallgau – Krepelschrofen – Panorama Trail – poss. Großer Wasserfall (Great Waterfall) and back – Maxhütte – Wallgau**

**Approach:** Wallgau, 866 m., holiday village on northern rim of the wide Isar plain with fine views of the Karwendel and Wetterstein mountains.
**Start:** Tennis courts, west of the village (Zugspitzstraße).
**Parking:** At the tennis courts.
**Walking Times:** Wallgau – Krepelschrofen 1 hr., Krepelschrofen – Maxhütte 1 hr.; return 40 min.; detour to Großer Wasserfall (there and back) 1¾ hrs.
**Difficulty:** Good footpaths.
**Highest Points:** Krepelschrofen, 1160 m., Maxhütte, 1022 m., belvedere at Großer Wasserfall, 920 m.
**Refreshments:** Maxhütte, cafés and restaurants at Wallgau.
**Of Interest:** The Großer Wasserfall.

*Right: Wallgau seen from the path to Krepelschrofen.*

For those who do not want a long walk, but would prefer a more leisurely ramble, we recommend the two hills above Wallgau. Then, anyone who is not satisfied with this can add on an excursion to the Great Waterfall. The Krepelschrofen is a truly picture-book walk; a narrow, charming path, impressive views, an open sunny forest and in the spring, an abundance of wild flowers. Later, across at the Maxhütte, the view over the broad Isar valley with the Wetterstein towering above, can be enjoyed over a glass of beer or a cup of coffee.

However, the Great Waterfall deserves more introduction. It is one of the most beautiful and interesting in the entire region. The powerful stream, which springs straight out of the rocks at its source, tumbles into the valley over countless rocky steps. All too soon, unfortunately, the path ends at a belvedere, which is too far away from the waterfall!

**From Wallgau up the Krepelschrofen:** The path up is always well marked by the number '19'. From the tennis courts to the Sonnleite and a short stretch upwards on the Panorama Trail. Then left and through the forest to a bench. Now on a narrower path through trees and glades to the highest point with view to the south. A few minutes farther north is a bench looking across towards the Walchensee.

**From Krepelschrofen to the Maxhütte:** Back down the path to the Panorama Trail and north along it to beyond the last houses of the village. Cross the main road and on the other side up along two extended curves to the Maxhütte.. Back on route '2' through the village to the car park.

**Excursion to the Great Waterfall:** One can drive to the edge of Wallgau village in the direction of Walchensee. Park at the junction of the road with the Panoramaweg (route '1'). From here it is possible to reach all three of today's goals. We follow '23' along a forestry road, eventually on a narrower path to a belvedere in the woods overlooking the waterfall opposite.

# 45 Simetsberg, 1840 m.

A lonely mountain high above the Walchensee

## Walchensee – Taferl – Tiroler Hut – Simetsberg; poss. descent via the Neuglägeralm

**Approach:** Walchensee, 806 m., holiday resort lying in meadows on the lake of the same name.
**Start:** From Walchensee take the road to Hotel "Einsiedl". 200 m. beyond a small road to Obernach branches right at an old quarry. Start across the Obernach bridge.
**Parking:** Beyond the bridge.

**Walking Times:** Car park – Simetsberg 3¾ hrs., poss. descent over the Neugläger- alm 2½ hrs.
**Difficulty:** No difficulties whatsoever. A sense of direction can be needed for the descent.
**Highest Point:** Simetsberg, 1840 m.
**Refreshments:** None.

*Walchensee with the Karwendel mountains beyond.*

One can awaken false hopes with the title "lonely mountain". Naturally, there are one or two mountaineers who do climb the Simetsberg. However, in this case "lonely" refers to the form and situation of the summit. The large, rounded dome stands utterly alone and isolated high above the deeply carved valleys and is connected to the remainder of the Krottenkopf range only by a deep saddle. It is an ascent which encourages contemplation – there are no dramatic views to admire. All the more beautiful then are the views from the summit, of the Walchensee, the Loisach at Eschenlohe, the Wetterstein, the Karwendel, ...

**The Normal Ascent:** Shortly after the aforementioned bridge the road branches. Follow the right fork up into the forest keeping left at each of the second and third junctions ("Taferl"/panel). We now reach the road which leads some 2 km. diagonally south across the wooded, eastern slopes of the Simetsberg. At the next junction turn sharply right. After several long curves a small valley to the east of the summit is reached. Climb up the valley gradually leaving the forest behind. At 1600 m. one reaches the wide, open plateau and moving left, onwards to the summit.

**Possible Descent** (not that easy to find!): Reaching out south below the summit there is an undulating grassy shoulder. From around the middle of the shoulder a footpath leads off south-west into a broad, broken saddle. Now south-east to Neuglägeralm and on east to the small saddle below the Neuglägerkopf. On a footpath – later a road – down to about 1200 m. where a further road is met. On this road back to the ascent route.

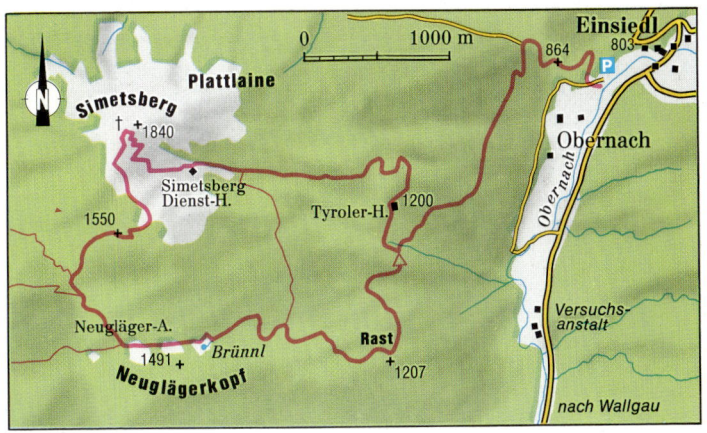

# 46 Jochberg, 1567 m.

The classic objective between the Walchensee and Kochelsee

**Kesselberghöhe – Jochberg; poss. Jachenau – Berg – Jocheralm – Jochberg – Kotalm – Hirschhörnlkopf – Jachenau**

**Approach:** Urfeld, 804 m., on the narrow northern shore of the Walchensee with its incongruously high appartment block.
**Start:** Kesselberghöhe, 658 m.
**Parking:** South or north of the pass.
**Walking Times:** 1¾ hrs.

**Difficulty:** Mountain footpaths with no particular difficulties.
**Highest Point:** Jochberg, 1567 m.
**Refreshments:** Jocheralm.
**Of Interest:** Views of Kochelsee and Walchensee.

The Jochberg is one of the most popular and well-known mountains in the Bavarian mountains. It is a summit with two different faces. From the south and viewed from across the Walchensee it appears as a rounded, grassy summit above forested slopes. However, from the north its summit falls away some 500 m. as a steep, scarred wall. The normal route up from the Kesselberghöhe is one of the shortest, but most interesting and rewarding mountain walks. Unfortunately, it is also one of the most heavily used. For those who would like to experience the Jochberg in a more individual and strenuous manner, we can offer a round tour during which very few people will be encountered.

**The Normal Ascent:** Directly out of the pass on a path through thick bushes at first, then young trees and open forest on to a spur. Now either – more attractively – along the ridge to the summit (the forest is soon left behind and open ground is reached); or, right to the Jocheralm and from there steeply

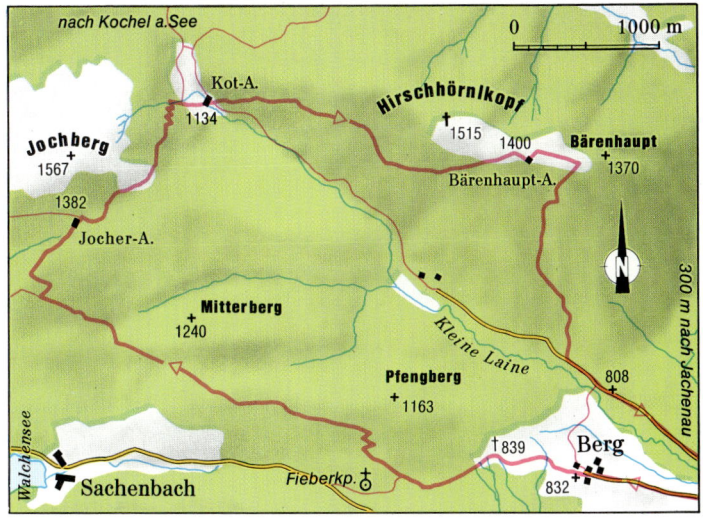

and almost straight up the beaten track to the summit cross. Especially fine views down on to the Kochelsee and the Walchensee.

**Round Tour Jochberg – Hirschhörnlkopf:** This sometimes lonely walk leads through wide expanses of forest. Nevertheless, views of the Walchensee and the surrounding peaks appear frequently. Five to six hours is normally needed for the complete walk which starts in the small hamlet of Berg, 832 m. (west of Jachenau).

Follow the forestry road which leads over to Sachenbach on Walchensee until just before the Fieberkapelle. Now steeply up and across the, in parts, steeply wooded slopes of the Pfengberg and Mitterberg. Then in long left curve up to the Jocheralm. From there on to the Jochberg and back to the pasture. Down to the north-west and across the meadows of the Kotalm. Right to the hut and just beyond it a track junction. Straight across the wooded slopes to the Bärenhauptalm on the east ridge of the Hirschhörnlkopf, 1515 m., – which can be reached in 20 min. Steep descent south to the edge of the forest and from there right across the start at Berg.

# 47 Herzogstand – Heimgarten

Observation pavilion and alpine "proving ground"

## Chair Lift – Fashrenbergkopf – Herzogstand; poss. Ridge Walk to Heimgarten and Descent via Ohlstädter Alm

**Approach:** Walchensee, 806 m., holiday resort lying in meadows on the lake of the same name.
**Start:** Top station of the chair lift directly below the Fahrenbergkopf, 1627 m. Bottom station at north end of the Walchensee.
**Parking:** Large car park at the bottom station (fee).
**Walking Times:** Lift – Herzogstand ¾ hr., Herzogstand – Heimgarten 1½ hrs.

**Difficulty:** To Herzogstand good paths. To Heimgarten – ridge walk with several rock sections (protected in parts). Sense of balance and surefootedness required.
**Highest Point:** Herzogstand, 1731 m; Heimgarten, 1790 m.
**Refreshments:** Herzogstandhäuser, Heimgarten Hut (below the summit).
**Of Interest:** Views down on to the Kochelsee and Walchensee.

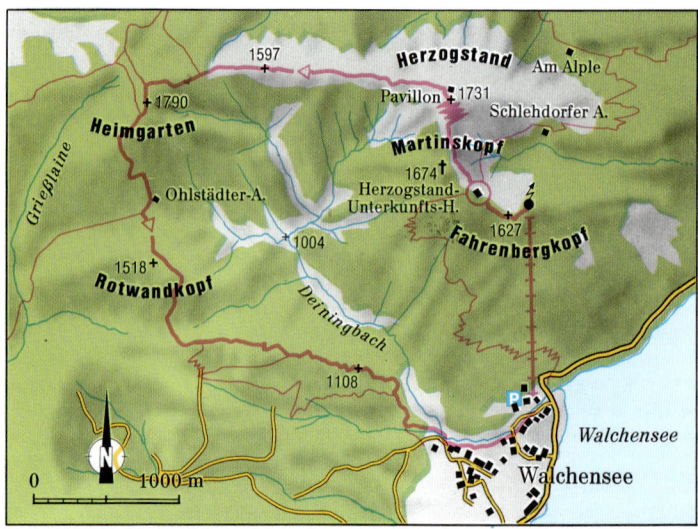

The Bavarian Kings appear to have found pleasure in especially fine views, otherwise there would not be a pavilion on the Herzogstand. From here the entire alpine foothills can be seen – as far out as the Ammersee and the Starnberger See. Neither would there be the well-prepared serpentine which transformes the way to the summit into an easy walk (from the top station!).

*The Herzogstand with a view of the Kochelsee.*

A quite other experience is presented by the sometimes rocky, knife-edged ridge across to the Heimgarten. Can there be a better opportunity to test one's alpine ability, surefootedness and sense of equilibrium?

**From the Lift to the Herzogstand:** From the top station across to the nearby Herzogstandhäuser. Then north around the Martinskopf and on long bends up to the summit.

**From the Herzogstand to Heimgarten:** This well used track cannot be missed. It leads for the most part along the knife-edged ridge; a few rock sections are avoided to the south. Finally up a slope to Heimgarten.

**Descent from Heimgarten to Walchensee:** Along the ridge south, then down across steep, partially wooded slopes to the Ohlstädter Alm. East along a reasonably level ridge below the Rotwandkopf and continue down the ridge to just above the valley floor. Now right through several outcrops and through almost level woods to the Rotwandgraben. At the junction left and alongside the stream back to the start.

# 48 Heimgarten, 1790 m.

Two routes up the local mountain in the Murnau region

**Ohlstadt – Schaumburg – Käseralm – Heimgarten – Rauheck – Wankhütte – Ohlstadt**

**Approach:** Ohlstadt, 664 m., beautifully situated holiday village between the Heimgarten and the Murnau moor.
**Start:** Upper edge of the village, 700 m.
**Parking:** Small car park above the houses.
**Walking Times:** Ohlstadt – Wankhütte 1¾ hrs., Wankhütte – summit 1½ hrs. Descent 2 hrs.
**Difficulty:** Good, sometimes steeper mountain paths.
**Highest Point:** Heimgarten, 1790 m.
**Refreshments:** Heimgartenhütte.

Five marked routes, each with its own individual character, climb upwards over the different sides of the Heimgarten. The paths from Ohlstadt offer much excitement and variety. At the same time they first meet the route described in Tour 47 at the summit; and one has a second opportunity to surmount its rounded, grassy crest. Even the two paths from Ohlstadt are entirely separate. The attraction of one is in the traversing of the Rauheck ridge, whilst on the other, one is able to admire the diverse, but invariably pinnacled landscape.

**Ascent via the Wankhütte:** Across the bridge and on the forestry road diagonally right over the meadows to the edge of the forest. Then a long section slanting right up through the woods and in the small valley of the Schwabwassergraben to the Wankhütte. Now left on to the ridge – only at Rauheck briefly on to the southern slope – up on to the Heimgarten massif. Remain on the ridge to the summit.

**Descent via the Käseralm:** Return to the northern edge of the ridge. Briefly along the northern ridge then steeply right and down into a gully below Rauchköpfl. Descent over a wide ledge then left to the Käseralm. Now on the path keeping west, passing Illing and through the forest to Ohlstadt.

*Left: Ohlstadt.*

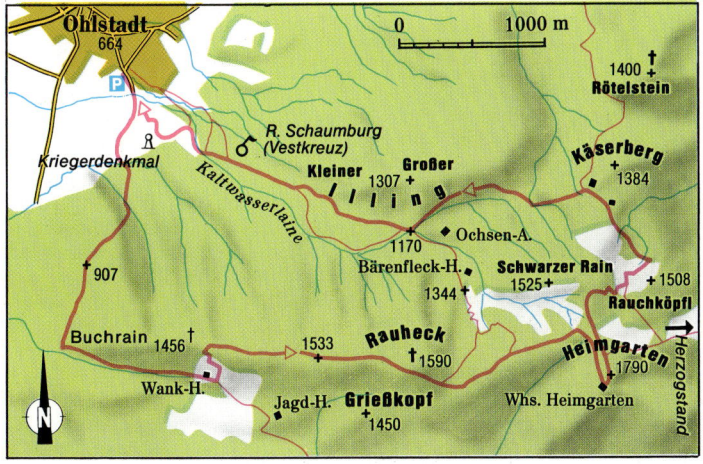

# 49 Rötelstein, 1400 m.

The last northern outpost

## Kreut (Glentleiten) – Auf der Platten – Rötelstein; poss. Heimgarten

**Approach:** Großweil, 620 m., village on the northern edge of the Alps near the motorway exit Murnau/Kochel.
**Start:** From Großweil 1.9 km. to the fascinating Farmhouse Museum at Glentleiten. 500 m. on to "Restaurant Kreut", 790 m., on a grassy ridge high above the Loisach. Magnificent views.
**Parking:** Ideal parking 200 m. beyond the restaurant on the edge of the forest.
**Walking Times:** 2 hrs. to the Rötelstein, poss. excursion to Heimgarten 1½ hrs.
**Difficulty:** To the foot of the mountain without difficulty. The summit is however steeper and rocky.
**Highest Point:** Rötelstein, 1400 m.
**Refreshments:** Only at the start "Restaurant Kreut".
**Of Interest:** Farmhouse Museum at Glentleiten.

*Right: Through open forest to the Rötelstein.*

A broad, forested area extends north beyond Heimgarten. Through its trees a mountain thrusts its summit and, although it too is almost submerged in trees, its name Rötelstein hints at the very nature of its construction. Here and there the rock shows through. The summit itself is rather like a cheeky, pointed rocky cap, but the north-western slopes plunge unusually steeply down into the valley. Consequently, this tour in the alpine foothills has a character all of its own. The almost flat and comfortable roads and paths, through the glades and forest, are followed by a short but steep, even strenuous, 200 min. climb to the summit cross.
However, the particular attraction is that it starts on the Glentleiten where the remarkable open-air Farmhouse Museum is situated – well worth a visit. Thus

this one excursion embraces local culture, a ramble through the woods and then a steep summit climb with all its interesting views.

**The Ascent:** On the forestry road through beech trees into a small valley, and on across clearings and among trees to a hunting lodge. Then at a junction left on the old path, firstly in open forest, later through an alley of young trees on to a shoulder. On to a prominent ridge which is followed to the north-west foot of the Rötelstein. Across the western slope with its rock outcrops to a forestry road. Follow it up for one bend, then on to an old forestry track which then becomes a footpath. Between the occasional spruce tree, crossing diagonally right and up into a saddle between the rocky western summit and the somewhat higher eastern one. Over a steep rounded ridge and finally across grass to the summit, with its large cross and summit book.

# 50 Kuhflucht

The valley of thundering water

**Farchant-Mühldörfl – Kuhfluchtgraben – Waterfall – Source; poss. Hoher Fricken – Frickenkar – Oberauer Steig – Mühldörfl**

**Approach:** Farchant, 672 m., holiday village just north of Garmisch-Partenkirchen in the Loisach valley.
**Start:** Mühldörfl – east of Farchant.
**Parking:** At Mühldörfl.
**Walking Times:** To the first waterfall 25 min. Onto the karst source ¾ hr. Ascent of Hoher Fricken 4 hrs. (from Mühldörfl).

**Difficulty:** Easy track to the first waterfall. Footpath to the rock slide and up the Hoher Fricken.
**Highest Points:** Waterfall, 790 m.; rock fall, 1150 m.; Hoher Fricken, 1940 m.
**Refreshments:** None.
**Of Interest:** The waterfalls and the Kuhflucht gorges.

Kuhflucht (flight of cows) – it sounds rather romantic and secretive. (Actually, it is merely the name of an area of meadow and woods at the foot of the Hoher Fricken.) But it suits the mood of today's excursion, for the Kuhflucht-

*Kuhflucht waterfalls near Farchant.*

bach is a remarkable phenomenon. Its entire valley is no longer then three kilometres. Nevertheless, the amount of water which, especially in the spring, plunges and thunders through it, is unbelievable. It has eaten deep into the brittle rock forming gorges and three fine waterfalls. There is an easy path to the first waterfall. Those with a little local knowledge climb higher to the site of a breathtaking, natural spectacle. Here, at a relatively recent rockfall, the mass of water hurtles out of the vertical rock like an artesian well.

**To the Kuhflucht Waterfall:** Through the village of Mühldörfl to the edge of the forest and through the remarkably open, green woods to the stream. Along its right bank up the valley to the lower fall.

**Onto the Rock Fall:** Over the iron bridge and up the steep slope on a narrow footpath, sometimes on the edge of the gorge, sometimes farther into the threes. At about 1100 m. (alt.) a path leads off left into the woods. Remain on the edge of the gorge (old markers) and climb straight up to the rock fall. Then right and up between somewhat loose boulders until the spring can be seen.

**Possible Summit Tour:** Remain on the path mentioned above which leads on up the very steep ground to the Hoher Fricken. Alternative descent: Along the ridge north-east into the saddle below the Bischof. Then left and down into the Fricken cirque and along the "Oberauer Steig" to just above the valley. At the junction left and along the edge of the meadows back to Farchant.

# Cross-Reference Index

The figure after the name of a place or mountain indicates the page.

Altenau 32
Ammerleite 31
Ammerwald, Hotel 56, 58
Arnspitze, Große 87
Asamklamm 14
Aufacker, Großer 24

Bäckenalmsattel 53
Bad Kohlgrub 22
Badersee 19
Bernadeinscharte 80
Biberwier 69, 70
Bichlbacher Alm 64
Bleik, Hohe 32
Blindsee 69
Brendlsee 73
Brunnenkopf 51
Brunnenkopfhäuser 50

Coburger Hut 73

Dammkar 103
Daniel 65
Dickelschwaig 49
Drachensee 73

Eckbauer 15, 82
Ederkanzel 16, 84
Ehrwald 72, 74
Ehrwalder Alm 15, 72, 75
Eibsee 19, 76
Eppzirler Alm 96
Eppzirlscharte 97
Eppzirltal 96
Ettal 10, 28, 42, 44, 46
Ettaler Manndl 28
Ettaler Mühle 45, 46
Ettaler Sattel 42, 44

Fahrenbergkopf 17, 114
Farchant 120

Feldernjöchl 75
Feldernkreuz 105
Fensterl 57
Ferchensee 19, 85
Fernpass 69
Fernpass-rock fall 13
Fernsteinsee 13
Fischbachalm 106
Freiungen-Höhenweg 97
Fricken, Hoher 121

Gabelschrofensattel 57
Gaistal 90, 92
Gaistalalm 92
Garmisch-Partenkirchen 10, 62, 78, 80, 82
Gartnertal 67
Gatterl 75
Gehrenspitze 89
Geierköpfe 58
Geroldsee 20
Gießenbach 96, 98
Gießenbachtal 42, 98
Glentleiten 11, 118
Grainau 76
Graswang 47, 48
Großweil 118
Grubigstein 69
Grubigsteinhaus 66, 68
Grubsee 20
Grünkopf 84
Gschwandkopf 15
Guglhör 17

Halbammer 32
Hammersbach 79
Handschuhspitzen 71
Hasentalkopf 53
Heimgarten 114, 116
Heldenkreuz 17
Hemermoosalm 15, 90

Herzogstand 114
Hirschhörnlkopf 113
Hochalm 15
Hochblasse 57
Hochland Hut 102
Hochplatte 57
Höllental 78
Höllentalanger Hut 78
Höllentalklamm (gorge) 13, 79
Höllkopf 70
Hölltörl 71
Hörnle 22
Hörnle Hut 14, 22
Hupfleitenjoch 79
Hüttlebachklamm (gorge) 105

Jachenau 113
Jochberg 112
Jocheralm 112

Kammerl 31
Karwendel cable car 102
Karwendelsteg 101
Klammspitze, Große 51
Knappenhäuser 78
Knorr Hut 75
Kochelsee 20
Kofel 36
Kolbenalm 36, 38
Kolbensattel 35, 39
Königssteig 37
Krähe 56
Kramer 62
Kranzberg, Hoher 16, 84
Krepelschrofen 108
Kreut 118
Kreuzeck 15
Krün 104, 106

Kuhalpenbachtal 48
Kuhflucht 14, 120

Laber 15, 26, 29
Lähn 64
Lakaiensteig 107

Lautersee 19, 85
Lermoos 64, 66, 68
Leutasch 88, 90, 92
Leutaschklamm (gorge) 14, 86
Linderhof 10, 47, 50, 52, 54
Linderspitze 103
Loisachblick 17
Lösertaljoch 53
Lottensee 19

Marienbergjoch 71
Max Hut 108
Mittagkopf 98
Mittenwald 10, 84, 86, 102
Mittersee 19
Möserer See 19
Munde, Hohe 93
Munde, Niedere 92
Murnau 11
Murnauer Moos 14

Neuweidtal 60
Niederbleik 33
Nördlinger Hut 94
Notkarspitze 44, 49

Oberammergau 10, 24, 26, 36, 38
Oberauer Steig 121
Ochsensitz 45
Ohlstadt 116
Open-air museum 11
Osterfelderkopf 80

Partnachklamm (gorge) 13, 81, 82
Pfeifferalm 15
Pflegersee 19
Plansee 17, 60
Pleisen Hut 100
Pleisenspitze 101
Pleisspitze 66
Predigtstuhl 90
Puittal 88
Pürschling 38, 40
Pürschlinghäuser 38, 40, 50
Pürzlkapelle 101

Rauth Hut 15
Rehbreinsattel 25
Reith 94
Reither Spitze 94
Riedbergscharte 87
Rießersee 19
Roggental 57
Romanshöhe 14, 24
Rötelstein 118
Rotmoosalm 90

Saulgrub 30
Scharnitz 100
Scharnitzjoch 89
Schartlehnerhaus 95
Scheibum 13, 30
Scheinbergjoch 53
Scheinbergspitze 54
Schlehdorf 10
Schleierfälle 13, 30
Schleifmühlenklamm 13, 34, 40
Schneefernerhaus 74
Schönberg 90
Schöttelkarspitze 105, 107
Seebenalm 73
Seebenfall 13
Seebensee 73
Seefeld 10, 94
Seefelder Joch 95
Seefelder Spitze 95
Seinsköpfe 104
Simetsberg 110
Soiener See 17
Soiernhäuser 106
Soiernseen 107
Solsteinhaus 97
Sommerbergjöchle 67

Sonnenberg 38
Staffelsee 20
Steckenberg 34
Steckenbergkreuz 34
Steinkarlkopf 103
Stepbergalm 62
Straußbergsattel 57
Stuibensee 81

Tajatörl, Hinteres 73
Teufelstal 59
Teufelstättkopf 40
Tonihof 16
Trauchberg, Hoher 32
Tuftlalm 64

Unterammergau 23, 34, 40
Unternogg 32
Urfeld 112

Vordergraseck 82

Walchensee (village) 110, 114
Walchensee (lake) 20
Wallgau 108
Wamberg 82
Wangalm 89
Wasserfall, Großer (Great Waterfall) 14, 109
Wellenberg (bathing facility) 17
Werdenfels, Ruin of 10
Wildsee 19
Wolfratshauser Hut 66

Zäunlkopf 98
Ziegelspitz 45
Zugspitze 74

# Glossary

Useful words which complement the Guide and Maps – and some abbreviations to be found on 1:50,000 Maps.

| | | | |
|---|---|---|---|
| Ache | river | Klettersteig | Via Ferrata – protected passage |
| Alm or Alp (A) | mountain pasture | | |
| Almhütte | summer farm | Kloster | monastery |
| Aussichtsturm (AT) | observation tower | Kopf | knoll, summit |
| Arzt | doctor | Krankenhaus (Khs) | hospital |
| Bach | stream | Moor | moor, marsh |
| Bahnhof (Bf) | station | Moos | moss or moor |
| Bergwacht | mountain rescue | Mühle | mill |
| Brücke | bridge | nach | to |
| Brunnen | well, spring | Pension | bed & breakfast |
| Diensthütte | forestry hut | Pfad | path |
| Fels | rocks | Quelle | source, spring |
| Ferner | glacier | Rinne | gully, groove |
| Friedhof | cemetery | Sattel | saddle |
| Fluss (ß) | river | Scharte | gap in ridge |
| Gasthaus | Restaurant, Public House, bar with meals | Scheune (Sch) | barn |
| | | Schulter | shoulder |
| | | Schuppen | barn |
| Geröll | scree | Schloß (ß) (Schl) | Castle |
| Gipfel | summit | Schlucht | gorge, canyon |
| Gipfelkreuz | summit cross | See | lake |
| Graben | stream, ditch, trench | Spitz(e) | peak |
| | | Sprungschanze | ski jump |
| Grat | ridge (rocky), edge | Steg | narrow path |
| | | Steig | mountain path |
| Grenze | border | Tal | valley |
| Grotte | grotto, cave | Teich | pond |
| Höhle | cave | Unterstand | shelter |
| Imbiss (ß) | snack, snack bar | Wald | woods, forest |
| Jausen-Station | snack bar | Wand | wall, face |
| Joch | pass, saddle | Weg | road, track, path |
| Jugendher_berge (JH) | youth hostel | Weiher (Whr) | weir |
| | | Wiese | meadow |
| Kamm | ridge | Wildfütterung | animal feeding |
| Kar | cirque | Wirtshaus (Whs) | see Gasthaus |
| Klamm | gorge | Zeltplatz | camp site |
| Kessel | bowl, basin | Zollamt | customs post |

# Gasthof Mühle Leutasch

That well-known Inn, "Gasthof zur Mühle" is conveniently situated on the footpath which winds from Mittenwald, through the Leutasch and Gais valleys, to Ehrwald. We offer our guests comfortable bedrooms in typical Tyrolean style, cosy public rooms, carefully prepared meals, selected wines and friendly hospitality.

**Gasthof Mühle  A-6105 Unterleutasch in Tirol  Telephone 0 52 14 / 67 12**
**Proprietors: The families Maurer and Lotter**